EXCELLENCE IN DIVERSITY

The Leverhulme Report

EXCELLENCE IN DIVERSITY

Towards a New Strategy
for Higher Education

SOCIETY FOR RESEARCH INTO HIGHER EDUCATION

The Society for Research into Higher Education
At the University, Guildford, Surrey GU2 5XH

First published 1983

© 1983 Society for Research into Higher Education

ISBN 0 900868 99 6

Printed by Camergraph Printing Limited, London EC1

FOREWORD

This report arises out of a wide-ranging programme of study organized by the Society for Research into Higher Education and financed by the Leverhulme Trust.

The term higher education conjures up many images. For some it is primarily a community of disinterested seekers after truth who are sometimes indistinguishable from the remote and ineffectual dons of Hilaire Belloc. Others see academic institutions as sources of intellectual power that can be focused according to current social priorities. Some imagine a wholesome but carefree environment for young adults before they embark on the serious business of life; others the inculcation of knowledge that will be directly profitable to students and to society. A more recent idea is that universities, polytechnics and colleges should be wider communities, with people dropping in from time to time throughout their lives.

Higher education is all of these things and more. Any selection of critical issues implies the adoption of a particular perspective. Ours derives from public policy. We are interested primarily in policies and policy mechanisms which will enable publicly financed institutions to perform well and to be seen to perform well. We have identified major issues that should be on the policy agenda during the next fifteen years whatever the nature of the governments, agencies and institutions that formulate and implement the detailed policies.

The full results of the programme of study are contained in nine specialist volumes summarized in the appendix to this report. Comments on earlier drafts of the report were made by the editors of the specialist volumes and by Richard Bird, Maurice Kogan, Peter Scott, John Thompson, Christopher Tipple and Ronald Tress. We are grateful to all of these individuals, but they are not responsible for what remains. A tenth volume, by Gareth Williams and Tessa Blackstone, is published at the same time as this report and reviews the programme of study as a whole.

Kenneth Berrill Norman Crowther-Hunt
Christopher Ball Kenneth Durham
Adrian Cadbury Alastair Pilkington
Michael Clapham Bruce Williams (subject to note of dissent p.34)

378
.41
E96

CONTENTS

I	BACKGROUND	1
II	SCOPE	2
III	AIMS OF THE STRATEGY	4
IV	ACCESS	4
V	CONTENT AND STRUCTURE OF COURSES	5
VI	PEER REVIEW AND THE MAINTENANCE OF ACADEMIC QUALITY	13
VII	RESEARCH	15
VIII	THE ACADEMIC PROFESSION	17
IX	THE BINARY SYSTEM	19
X	THE ROLE OF GOVERNMENT	22
XI	THE INSTITUTIONS	26
XII	IMPROVING ACADEMIC LEADERSHIP	29
XIII	SUMMARY	31
	NOTE OF DISSENT	34
	APPENDIX: A SUMMARY OF EVIDENCE	37
	ACKNOWLEDGEMENTS	78

I

BACKGROUND

Today's children will inherit a world of high technology, and they will probably spend less of their lives in paid employment than any previous generation. While at work, however, they will need to be more efficient and more productive than ever before. In work and in leisure their well-being will depend on their knowledge, skills and creativity. Universities, polytechnics and colleges are not the only social institutions involved in producing and disseminating knowledge, developing skills and cultivating creativity, but their role is a crucial one.

For some years there has been no coherent national policy for higher education. It is nearly twenty years since Robbins devised a strategy of expansion which worked well until a combination of stagnating demand from school-leavers for traditional courses, severe economic stringency and impending population decline undermined it. Robbins proposed, and for many years governments accepted, that demand from school-leavers who were qualified and willing to enter degree-level courses should largely determine the provision of places in higher education. The criterion, although still a valid starting point, no longer gives satisfactory policy guidance. The DES discussion document **Higher Education into the 1990s** (1978) drew attention to demographic changes. It showed that after several years in which the *percentage* of young persons qualifying for higher education had not risen above about 14 per cent, the *number* of 18-year-old school-leavers would reach a peak of 941,000 in 1982/3 and fall by over a third to 622,000 by 1995/6. [1] There will be substantial excess capacity by the early 1990s unless universities, polytechnics and colleges can adapt to new tasks and to the needs of new types of student. They must be capable of responding to academic developments and to fresh demands from society. They must be in the forefront of technology, both initiating and evaluating it. However, little additional capacity will be created. New developments must come from adaptation, not expansion.

Much of the work of colleges, universities and polytechnics is intrinsically valuable but this does not preclude the need for some public accountability. Major industries have declined when demand has changed and enterprises have been unable to adapt. Response to changing demand need not be passive acceptance of external circumstances. Education is properly concerned with influencing public attitudes. Nevertheless, the case for public expenditure on higher education must be based on benefits for the nation, not merely on the convenience or interest of members of the higher education community. One of the main aims of this report is to suggest changes which would make more visible the contributions of higher education to the economy and to society.

Expenditure has to be restrained in an activity that must remain largely within the public sector and compete for resources with other social and educational services. Relief from the pressure of demand from school-leavers following the dramatic fall in the 18-year-old population will provide opportunities for the establishment of new patterns of courses within stable budgets. The strategy outlined in this report would encourage the development of a network of vigorous, efficient and cost-effective institutions, each excellent in its own range of activities, each imbued with a strong sense of academic purpose and responsive to the needs of a wider society. The main theme is an endorsement of diversity. This requires strong institutions and multiple criteria for policy formulation and resource allocation.

II

SCOPE

For some purposes it is convenient to aggregate all forms of education for students beyond the minimum school-leaving age. Sometimes it is more appropriate to combine all education for adults above the age of 18. Both approaches to a definition of higher education have value. There is reciprocity between higher education and the schools, and an infinite gradation between the most academic higher education and the most utilitarian further education. There has been a welcome growth of political interest in continuing education and considerable expansion of basic education courses for adults. Nevertheless, *higher* education remains a distinguishable part of post-compulsory and post-secondary education. The Robbins Report 'concentrated on the universities in Great Britain and those

---

[1] Recent estimates show that after taking into account differences in the birthrate in the two main social classes identified by the Office of Population Censuses and Surveys, the number of school-leavers with two 'A' level passes in England is likely to fall by 23% between now and 1995/6 (DES **Statistical Bulletin** 6/83 April 1983).

colleges, within the purview of the Ministry of Education and the Scottish Education Department, that provide courses for the education and training of teachers or systematic courses of further education beyond the Advanced level of the General Certificate of Education (or higher grade of the Scottish Certificate of Education) or beyond the Ordinary National Certificate or its equivalent.' Allowing for a few administrative and terminological changes since 1963, that is the definition we adopt. It has the advantage of focusing on identifiable institutions and on educational activities which are for the most part clearly recognizable as being above the level normally achieved by secondary school pupils. In concrete terms the definition embraces at present 50 universities, 30 polytechnics, 14 Scottish central institutions, 64 other colleges and institutes of higher education, together with some of the courses in more than 300 colleges of further education.

Even when thus circumscribed a wide range of activities is included in the idea of higher education - from pure research at the frontiers of knowledge to short practical courses below the level of a first degree. Part-time study, courses that are shorter and sometimes less intellectually demanding than Honours degrees, consultancy for industry, commerce and government, and much other public service are all elements of a modern system of higher education.

Because of this heterogeneity, general statements of the purposes of higher education as a whole are of little use. There is, however, a need for clear understanding of the aims of particular activities. Courses need to have objectives which can be communicated both to students and to the employers of graduates. Research needs to be grounded in some academic or social purpose even if its outcomes cannot be predicted. Universities, polytechnics and colleges must have a sense of mission if they are to survive the challenges of the next two decades.

This report does not attempt to solve immediate detailed problems. It explores issues from a broader and longer perspective. However, it would not have been helpful to attempt to peer so far into the future that current realities were ignored. If too short a view runs the risk of practical problems overwhelming issues of principle, too long a view enables wishful thinking to dominate both principle and practice.

---

[1] Includes 44 universities financed by the UGC and 6 other chartered bodies.

III

AIMS OF THE STRATEGY

Our strategy has eight main aims:

a   To provide opportunities for all who are able to benefit from some form of higher education and to encourage access from a broader social spectrum than at present.

b   To reduce undue specialization in secondary education and the initial years of higher education.

c   To create a framework within which the quality of teaching and research can be maintained. at a time when underlying demographic trends will make competition for resources difficult.

d   To stimulate research and other academic activities not directly linked to student numbers.

e   To encourage institutions to prepare realistic development plans.

f   To increase the capacity of universities, polytechnics and colleges to respond positively to changing academic, social, economic and industrial needs.

g   To promote efficiency in the use of resources.

h   To create a framework for policy and management studies that will help leaders of academic institutions meet the challenge of adaptation without growth.

IV

ACCESS

British students tend to be young and to be concentrated in full-time courses. High academic quality is associated with careful selection of entrants, favourable staff/student ratios and good physical facilities. The 1960s expansion of higher education was based on a known and trusted pattern that had produced an excellent learning environment for a minority. **Access to Higher Education**[1] shows how concentrated this provision remains, despite some welcome expansion of part-time and non-degree courses outside the universities. A central concern for the future is whether this pattern remains the best way of providing for a larger and more varied student population. Is too much of our higher education effort concentrated on full-time Honours degree courses for school-leavers? Do we discourage too many students whose interests and needs are different?

Robbins drew attention to marked differences in participation rates between different social groups, and these remain. To this has been added, since the time of Robbins, the problem of apparently low participation by some ethnic minorities, though the evidence is scanty and needs to be improved. The overall proportion of students who are women rose for several years but declined between the mid 1970s and the early 1980s. Considerable disparities persist in participation rates between different regions of the country. Such discrepancies should not be accepted as an inescapable feature of higher education. There should be renewed efforts to diagnose their causes and remedy any educational and social deficiencies of which they prove to be symptoms.

V

CONTENT AND STRUCTURE OF COURSES

The comments in this section apply particularly to the Honours degree courses which are still dominant in the universities. Though public sector institutions have many more students doing different types of courses, the full-time Honours degree is prevalent there also. In a recent publication Lord Robbins [2] claims that the expansion of specialized degree courses in the 1960s and 1970s was not intended by his Committee. He argues for considerable changes in present arrangements and refers to the 'iniquitous habit of ultra specialization at tender ages. ...' 'As regards specialization at

---

[1] Unless otherwise stated, all references are to the SRHE Leverhulme volumes summarized in the Appendix (p.37-77).

[2]Robbins, Lionel (1980) **Higher Education Revisited** Blackwell.

the later stages of schooling, we are completely out of step with the rest of free societies ... and run the acute danger of turning out a race of citizens virtually uncomprehending each other as regards the broader topics of civilised talk. ...' 'Extreme specialization suitable for research scholarship or professional training should be reserved for the graduate schools.'

In **The Arts and Higher Education** it is argued that excessive specialization occurs because the main link between schools and higher education is the public examination. It is, of course, possible to envisage different kinds of examination and assessment of students during and at the end of secondary education. However, it seems unlikely that the long-running debate on the reform of the 'A' level examination will be brought to a satisfactory conclusion unless initial courses in higher education itself demand less specialization.

A wide-ranging debate is needed about the content of undergraduate courses in the light of contemporary needs. One reason for proposing a radical reform of the structure of undergraduate education is to try to succeed where expansion accompanied by exhortation failed and to break into the circle of excessive specialization in secondary and higher education.[1]

The specialized Honours degree has intrinsic merits. It is centred on the idea of an academic discipline: a coherent body of knowledge or range of subject matter that 'holds together' and provides recognized methods of analysis. If successful, it trains students in a particular way of thinking and provides them with an epistemology that has been legitimated by the wider intellectual community. However, there are also advantages in properly integrated degree schemes in which students are able to experience the methods of thought of several disciplinary perspectives. There is no reason why everything in an undergraduate curriculum should be taught in great depth. Breadth and the ability to integrate different ideas have intellectual as well as practical value. Students need to be shown how subjects interact and how different disciplines may be applied to help solve practical problems or policy issues. In their study of British academics Halsey and Trow found that well over half of their sample of university teachers considered it a valid criticism of the English universities that they over-emphasized the single-subject Honours degree.[2] Robbins pointed out that many students are uncertain what course they want to follow when they enter higher education and do not have a clear idea what career they wish to pursue when they leave. In the probable employment conditions of the

---

[1] Traditionally, Scotland has been exempted from such strictures. However, in an important recent book, **Reconstructions of Secondary Education** (1983), Gray, McPherson and Raffe show that in Scotland there is a trend in upper secondary education towards specialization in a narrow range of subjects.

[2] Halsey, A.H. and Trow, M. (1971) **The British Academics** Faber.

1980s and 1990s very specialized first degrees are likely to be even less appropriate than they were in the 1960s.

Ashworth[1] has recently proposed that higher education should aim to cultivate in undergraduate students:

a   'the capacity to acquire and manipulate knowledge and thereby to develop what the Robbins Committee called "the general powers of the mind";

b   the capacity to appreciate, to value and to make judgement of what is beautiful, of good repute and fit for its purpose. This involves the training of feeling and emotions as well as implying a moral and ethical framework within which (a) above is done;

c   the capacity to formulate and solve concrete problems and to make, design, organize, produce or construct useful projects and services;

d   the capacity to co-ordinate with others; to value communion as well as competition with one's peers.'

Most students, employers of graduates and indeed most teachers in higher education would agree with this list. How far higher education is achieving such aims can, however, be questioned. Are undergraduate courses continuing to produce graduates who have spent too long acquiring knowledge over too narrow an area? Have these graduates been given sufficient opportunity to exercise aesthetic or ethical judgements? Have they had enough experience of problem formulation? Have they been encouraged throughout their secondary and higher education to value individualistic competition rather than co-operation with their peers in joint intellectual ventures? In a submission to this study members of the Committee of the Standing Conference of Employers of Graduates claimed that

'... in their degree courses graduates must already have been instilled with the capacity to learn for themselves, to adapt, to solve problems, to comunicate effectively with others, and to commit themselves to the broad objectives of an organisation. All these factors can be enhanced in the early years of employment but an employer can only build on the potential he finds; he cannot create a new person. Employers sometimes feel that higher education could have done more to prepare the ground.'

---

[1] Ashworth, J.M. (1982) Reshaping higher education in Britain **Journal of the Royal Society of Arts** October.

Four of the SRHE Leverhulme volumes make proposals for new patterns of initial courses of study, strongly emphasizing the need for flexibility. **Agenda for Institutional Change** recommends that 'the establishment of two-year degrees should be considered both by the universities and the CNAA.' Similar proposals have been made by many authors since the idea was mooted in 1969 by Sir Brian Pippard.[1] In recent months there has been increased public discussion of proposals for a pattern of courses linked by a basic initial course of two years of full-time study (or part-time equivalent) rather than the three or four-year full-time Honours degree which forms the linchpin of the present system. The apparent inability of many institutions of higher education to offer students anything worthwhile in less than three years of full-time study certainly invites questions.

Five main arguments can be put forward in support of less specialized two-year initial courses.

i   Shorter initial courses accompanied by genuine possibilities of credit transfer between institutions and a variety of subsequent options would permit greater flexibility and give individual students more opportunity to tailor their higher education to meet their own particular needs and interests.

ii   Relatively short basic courses linking more than one disciplinary perspective but of good academic quality would help to overcome the problem of early over-specialization and would be suited to the needs of many students and many employers in a system of mass higher education.

iii Such courses could be widely available in a variety of institutions and would thus remove a serious obstacle to access, particularly for adults and working-class students (especially girls), who do not have a strong tradition of leaving home to go to college.

iv For some students the prospect of a two-year rather than a three-year initial commitment might be less daunting.

v   Courses could be provided at a lower average cost per student year if they were less specialized. There would be fewer uneconomic small courses. A greater proportion of students could live at home. More people would have some experience of higher education for any given level of expenditure. However, whether the net effect is more or less total expenditure depends on the number of students who would proceed to higher-level courses.

---

[1] Pippard, Brian (1969) The educated scientist **Physics Bulletin**.

Three possible versions of two-year initial courses of study have been proposed: more intensive first degrees of the existing type, a new type of non-degree qualification in some institutions, and a new type of initial degree in all institutions.

Agenda for Institutional Change argues that Honours degree standards could be met by lengthening the academic year, which many outside higher education would see as a desirable reform in itself. Staff research and study time could be protected through study leave arrangements. This is the pattern that has been adopted at the University of Buckingham. Such an approach would save little money if the provision for staff study leave resulted in periods of absence corresponding to existing vacations. More intensive use of buildings and equipment would be partly offset by their unavailability for activities such as conferences. Two-year intensive Honours degree courses would make it difficult to reduce specialization in many subjects.

Another proposal is to treat two-year courses as an alternative qualification alongside the Honours degree. This has been tried in the form of the Diploma of Higher Education, which was introduced in 1973, but has little chance of success if traditional three and four-year Honours degree courses supported by mandatory student grants continue to dominate provision in universities and polytechnics.

The third possibility is a different type of initial degree qualification in all institutions. One qualification, previously widespread, which has become much less common in England[1] is the Pass degree. In Scotland this remains the course for which students initially enrol and the qualification with which about a half of them finally graduate.[2] It is interesting that in Scotland participation rates are considerably higher than in England. A two-year Pass degree could be the link which brings together several ideas currently under discussion for shorter, less specialized, more flexible, more widely available basic courses. Entry requirements could be broader than those required at present for admission to specialized Honours courses. The 18+ examination could be reformed to accommodate more subjects which need not necessarily all be studied to the same level. For older students a range of other qualifications, including various kinds of work experience supported by interview or aptitude tests, would be appropriate. There is a case for a national system of preparatory courses and selection procedures appropriate for adults wishing to return to higher education: the Open College

---

[1] Except in medicine and, to a much lesser extent, engineering. The Open University also offers an ordinary (Pass level) degree.
[2] The traditional Scottish pattern is for students to enter higher education one year earlier than in England, so the first year of the three-year Pass degree course is in some respects the equivalent of the English 2nd-year sixth. Our suggestions would leave this largely unchanged.

Federation of the North West, involving Lancaster University, Preston Polytechnic and several further education colleges, is one model that might readily be adapted to accommodate the new pattern of courses.

Pass degree courses might normally adopt a rather broad approach to a disciplinary area, preparing the way for subsequent specialization; they should not, we stress, be a mish-mash of anything and everything. They could vary quite considerably in the extent of specialization and generalization. Some could be related to particular occupations, possibly with the qualification designated Bachelor of the occupation concerned. The availability and content of occupation-related degrees would need to be determined, as are most equivalent non-degree courses at present, according to estimates of national and regional need in collaboration with appropriate professional bodies and employers.

In many professional areas such as engineering and medicine, considerable specialist study would of course be necessary beyond the Pass degree. However, some broadening of curricula in such fields during the first two years of study would in the end produce better engineers and doctors, because their education would give them a better grasp of the relationship between their professional skills and the activities and interests of other people with whom they come into contact professionally and in their lives generally.

A central issue in any consideration of a pattern of courses based on shorter periods of initial study is what opportunities they would open up to students. If three-year Honours degrees were squeezed into two years few changes would be needed in the pattern of postgraduate study. If two-year Diploma of Higher Education courses were expanded alongside existing three and four-year degrees, the key issue would be the terms on which students completing the diploma could transfer to full degree courses.

However, a two-year Pass degree would require radical rethinking of both undergraduate curricula and the pattern of postgraduate courses. A student obtaining a Pass degree would need to have, first, a credential that had some intrinsic value and was recognized both by employers and by those who control entry to subsequent specialized courses. One route could be similar to the existing Honours and research degree track. After obtaining a Pass degree some students would finish their higher education at least for a time. Others would proceed to a one-year Honours course enabling them to go on to a higher degree. Another route could lead to one, two and three-year courses related to specific occupations. Universities and polytechnics in particular would need to provide realistic opportunities at Honours and postgraduate levels for students transferring from other institutions. A possible difficulty is that they would have a rather short period in which to settle down to useful work in their new institution. These problems are not insuperable. There is already transfer to one-year courses at postgraduate diploma and Masters degree levels. Certainly any widespread system of credit transfer would require collaboration between institutions, including, for example, the organization of summer schools.

In total, three layers of higher-level study should be built on to the basic two-year course. The first should be courses leading either to Honours degrees or to occupation-related postgraduate diplomas. After this, further one-year courses should lead to a variety of qualifications at Masters level. They might be broadly divided into those which were academic and research-based and those linked to particular occupations. There would, however, be a great deal of variation in both layers, according to subject and vocational training. For example, in some areas of study the two layers might be combined into a two-year Masters degree. Finally, the third layer of postgraduate study would lead to doctorates, which again might be divided into research degrees and high-level vocational qualifications.

Research degrees and research training need special consideration. The traditional PhD is likely to come under increasing pressure to change as academic jobs remain scarce, restricting one of its main career avenues. **The Future of Research** recommends that

> '... the PhD should be seen more as a training experience than as a major contribution to knowledge. There should be more explicit training in research methodology and more opportunities for research done as part of a team. The experience should encourage flexibility and enable the researcher to be able to move between areas of work within the same discipline. ...'

The structure of postgraduate courses outlined above could help meet this aim. A PhD graduate would normally have completed four distinct courses of higher education—an initial two-year Pass degree, the specialized Honours year, a predominantly taught course of research training at Masters level, and finally a period of supervised independent study leading to a thesis. Each of these stages would provide a qualification with intrinsic value as well as preparing for a higher-level qualification. A similar four-stage pattern might be followed in many professional areas of study, with the top qualification being a doctorate in the associated academic area of study.

This summary does not cover every eventuality. In particular, it is couched largely in terms of full-time study. Most courses could have part-time variants and it would be easier for students to integrate periods of full-time and part-time study. For example, the practice of adult students doing an initial course at the Open University followed by a full-time specialized Honours year or diploma course elsewhere could become more widespread. At present three and four-year courses predominate and a limited amount of flexibility and variety is provided by parallel, and usually lower-status, non-degree courses, mostly in the public sector. There is little contact between degree and non-degree streams. A pattern of higher education courses based on a core of two years of study leading to a variety of subsequent options would increase flexibility as well as having academic and economic advantages.

It would not be possible to impose a particular structure of courses on autonomous universities. Public sector institutions are subject to more external leverage but here, too, major change has a greater chance of success if initiated from within. However, present financial arrangements, particularly those for student grants, discourage institutions from offering, and students from seeking, courses other than those leading to full-time Honours degrees. In general, finance could be used more purposefully as an instrument encouraging response to changing circumstances. The resource allocation criteria of funding agencies should encourage a flexible pattern of courses. For example, the unit of resource per student could be higher for third and subsequent years of study to reflect the higher costs of more specialized courses and to encourage the acceptance of transfer students. Furthermore, if means-tested mandatory grants were available to all students on the two-year initial courses but financial support for subsequent courses were based on other criteria, students would be encouraged to seek, and universities, polytechnics and colleges to provide, courses that could be completed within two years.

There should be financial support for students on higher-level courses. However, the criteria should be different. Five categories of support can be envisaged. The first would be scholarships for those who are exceptionally talented. Most research council awards at present are of this type and they would probably remain largely confined to students doing research degrees. The second would be grants in areas of special national or local need in which too few students of suitable quality were coming forward. The third would be sponsorship of individual students by employers, including employers in the public sector. The fourth would consist of special grants to enable those suffering from long-term structural unemployment as a result of technological change to update their skills or acquire new ones. The fifth would be a government-backed loan scheme enabling students on higher-level courses to invest in their own futures.

The issue of loans is thoroughly reviewed in **Resources and Higher Education** which makes proposals for a mixed system of grants and loans; a similar proposal is made in **Access to Higher Education**. A general conclusion is that, provided repayment arrangements are geared to realistic assessments of ability to pay, student support through loans is at least as equitable as support through means-tested grants. The success of loan schemes in a number of countries suggests that administrative problems can be overcome.

VI

PEER REVIEW AND THE MAINTENANCE OF ACADEMIC QUALITY

In a period of adaptation without growth there is a danger that quality could be compromised as institutions compete for students and resources. In **Higher Education and the Labour Market** and **Access to Higher Education**, Freeman and Trow have given examples of some of the damaging effects of competition between institutions in the United States. Prime responsibility for standards must rest with the higher education community. Academic freedom has intrinsic value. Nevertheless, there is a legitimate external interest, and the higher education community benefits when its quality is clearly visible. Government has responsibilities on behalf of the rest of society, but at the heart of arrangements for the maintenance of standards must be a recognition that teaching and research are skilled professional activities and they are rarely done efficiently if they are subject to intrusive external control.

At present the Council for National Academic Awards (CNAA) validates degree courses outside the universities. The Business and Technician Education Council (BTEC) performs a similar function for non-degree courses. Her Majesty's Inspectorate and local authorities also have a role in non-university institutions, particularly in teacher education. In universities, teaching quality is for the most part internally regulated, but the subject committees of the University Grants Committee (UGC) are concerned to ensure that departments have the capacity for the academic work they should be doing. In research there is rigorous control of quality through formal and informal networks of peer review of grant applications and published work. Teaching in both universities and other institutions is subject to an uncoordinated system of external examining of students. Finally, there is the accreditation of courses by professional bodies.

While such mechanisms have helped to maintain quality, there are doubts about how well suited they are to cope with the pressures of adaptation without growth. Peer review in research is thorough and the results of academic research are open to public and peer-group scrutiny. However, questions can be asked about most of the others. The CNAA and BTEC have dealt mainly with the review of new institutions and courses but must now focus on the adaptation of existing activities when resources are not expanding. The CNAA is aware of the problems. It has gradually been moving from a body exercising power of veto or modification of new courses to one seeking to maintain standards in partnership with polytechnics and colleges. Reservations about the Inspectorate concern the ability of a small corps of individuals, however able, to make a significant contribution to the maintenance of quality in the thousands of activities that comprise higher education. In universities, concern has been expressed about evaluation by UGC subject committees which are an integral part of a dominant funding body. The lack of open criteria on which the UGC bases its judgements is also questioned as well as whether it is sufficiently well staffed to undertake anything other than cursory and in some cases arbitrary reviews. The system of external examining comes in for criticism in **Professionalism and Flexibility in Learning**, arising mainly from the great variety of practice with regard to the selection and responsibilities of examiners and doubts about whether in general they can exert a significant influence on teaching and assessment of students.

Courses that prepare students for particular occupations must satisfy professional requirements, and experienced members of the professions must be in a position to judge whether they do. However, a professional body has a responsibility to judge new developments in terms primarily of effects on the profession rather than benefits to graduates trying to join it. This can mean excessively rigid control of entry. The debate about an engineering council has raised many of the issues. The relationship between the requirements of professional bodies and the provision of courses in higher education institutions needs special study which we were not able to undertake.

In general, there are marked differences of practice between universities and other institutions. Polytechnics and colleges are subject to a network of outside influences and controls from the CNAA, BTEC, the regional advisory councils, the local authorities, and HMIs, while universities respond only to those external voices they choose to heed. During the course of our study two broad views emerged. One was that the non-university institutions should have less external intervention in their academic affairs; the other was that universities should have more.

There is certainly a case for some convergence of practice. Most polytechnics and colleges of higher education are now mature institutions with experienced senior staff: they should be subjected only to controls that are strictly necessary for the maintenance of academic quality and the efficient use of national resources. On the other hand, along with some universities they may in the future find themselves under pressure to compromise academic quality in attempting to maintain student numbers or earn income from other sources. Some co-ordination of arrangements is desirable to try to ensure, for example, that academic standards for similar activities do not diverge too widely between institutions, that students are not misled about the nature of courses they select, that they are assessed fairly and in an equivalent manner throughout higher education, that the requirements of professional bodies are not oppressive for individual students or institutions, that criteria for student credit transfer are efficient and fair and that funding bodies are well informed about the academic merits of different activities. We believe that the universities should establish an academic review body with these broad functions and that this body should collaborate with the CNAA, with the possibility that in due course the two bodies might combine.

The issue is not whether arrangements for external quality control should be established: much already exists and funding bodies will be increasingly drawn into quality comparisons between institutions. The essential issues are whether existing arrangements should be made more systematic, whether the administrative distinction between universities and other institutions should correspond to such a sharp distinction in methods of academic regulation, whether judgements about the academic quality of institutions should be made openly, and whether the regulation of arrangements for quality should be under academic or administrative and financial control.

VII

RESEARCH

Institutions of higher education contribute directly to the national capacity for fundamental and applied research and train the next generation of researchers. In doing so they contribute to the solution of social and economic problems and help in the attainment of other cultural objectives. There are doubts whether these functions are at present being performed as well as they ought to be; mechanisms of research finance which were established in a period of expansion and economic buoyancy may not be well adapted to present and future needs. The financial constraints of the 1970s were associated with a more than proportionate reduction in research expenditure in universities. A central theme of **The Future of Research** is the danger that the much more severe financial stringency of recent years and the decline in the number of school-leavers will do irreparable damage to the nation's research effort.

On the central issue of whether research and good undergraduate teaching are indivisible **The Future of Research** is agnostic. There are some complementarities in both personnel and equipment, which make it convenient for some kinds of research to be undertaken in the same institutions as some kinds of teaching. Obviously the happiest outcome for all occurs when excellent research workers are also excellent teachers. However, good teachers can be poor researchers and vice versa; and teaching and research can compete for the time of staff and for equipment and facilities. The book draws the conclusion that a clearer conceptual separation of the teaching and research functions would help to protect research. It recommends that university funding should distinguish between undergraduate teaching and general support of scholarship on one hand and postgraduate teaching and research on the other. It suggests specifically that the funding of research should be linked in part to designated research centres at each institution; and in making general grants funding bodies should be influenced by success in obtaining specific project funds.

A corollary is that any institution where research is seen as a significant activity would need to have a research policy determining the balance of its effort between subject areas, between research and research training, and between different forms of applied and pure research. The explicit statement of research priorities will present institutions with difficult decisions. That is the price of independence. The alternative is to have such decisions made externally, for example by allocating a larger proportion of resources through the research council mode of specific grants for defined areas of research.

Agnosticism about the direct links between undergraduate teaching and research leads to the conclusion that different institutions will have a different balance of teaching and research, and that in areas where equipment is expensive or where there are other significant economies of scale in research there must inevitably be some concentration of effort. Some research groups which in the past might have had a legitimate expectation of growing to a viable size as their institutions expanded will not now do so. It is doubtful, however, whether the distinction between universities and other institutions provides clear guidance on institutions where research should be encouraged. **The Future of Research** endorses the concept of polytechnics having a special role in applied research and recommends that each polytechnic should have an explicit research policy. A shift of resources towards a programme-funding mode for research (see Section XI, p.26) would enable polytechnics to compete on more favourable terms for research grants.

The issue of research and research training in the arts and humanities is raised in **The Future of Research** and in **The Arts and Higher Education.** The main policy issue is whether a separate research council is needed for the arts and humanities and, if so, what its scope should be. Both reports are coutiously sympathetic to the idea. The implications of setting up such a council should be studied by the Department of Education and Science and other interested bodies such as the British Academy and the Arts Council.

VIII

THE ACADEMIC PROFESSION

The efficiency and enthusiasm of members of the academic profession must be maintained during a long period of adaptation without growth. Effective professional development policies and open styles of management can help to maintain morale; but it is necessary to ensure that some well-qualified graduates are regularly appointed to academic posts; that all members of universities, polytechnics and colleges are able to contribute usefully to the work of their institutions; that those who occupy positions of responsibility retain their capacity to shoulder their responsibilities; that there is some mobility of staff; and that students have opportunities to benefit from the expertise of people with recent experience outside higher education.

In the contraction of recent years many members of staff have taken early retirement. This, following the rapid expansion of the 1960s, means that a high proportion of those remaining are now in mid-career, and in the normal course of events retirement will be very low for several years, a circumstance likely to make it difficult for institutions to adapt at a time when the need for adaptation will be great. Early retirement schemes will continue to be needed. However, reduction of the average length of working life through long-term early retirement has major implications for pension schemes which will have to be faced by government, by institutions and by the academic profession. At the other end of the scale it is not desirable to subject very able young graduates to excessively long periods on temporary contracts before they are assured of reasonable prospects of an academic career. As well as being hard on individuals, many of whom are establishing homes and families along with their careers, long periods of probation and temporary employment could put higher education institutions at a disadvantage in competing with other employers for the most talented young people.

In universities the issue of lifetime tenure cannot be avoided. It is unfortunate that this issue has come to the forefront of political debate at a time of severe financial stringency because the issues involved are not primarily financial. The need for some job security in defending intellectual activity from undue external pressure must be recognized. Yet the importance of lifetime tenure for all teachers as a defence of academic freedom can be exaggerated. In particular, temporary staff waiting for tenured posts to become available may have doubts about some of the claims. Research staff, even at senior levels, rarely have tenure. Staff in public sector institutions are covered by normal contracts of employment. There is little evidence that this has inhibited their ability to express their views or to determine the content of their own teaching or research activity. Furthermore, tenure in itself is by no means impregnable in institutions heavily dependent on a single source of public funds. There is a strong case for treating university teachers like their research and public sector colleagues and protecting their rights through employment protection legislation (which did not exist until relatively recently) rather than seeking to maintain lifetime tenure as the standard form of university teaching appointment.

It is difficult to determine how well an academic is carrying out his teaching activities except in cases of serious dereliction of responsibility. Management procedures are needed to help encourage good academic practice. In many areas of professional employment there are now annual appraisals of performance, and such reviews could usefully be introduced in higher education. Performance reviews may be inappropriate for senior academics, yet particularly serious damage can result from their incompetence. The widespread extension of arrangements for fixed terms of appointment for senior positions of responsibility is desirable. Appointments could be renewable, but open to competition when an individual's term of office ends.

A growing number of academics have worked in only one institution. Not all mobility is fruitful: some continuity has advantages, and there are excellent teachers and researchers who spend their whole lives in one place. Nevertheless, in general, universities, polytechnics and colleges are invigorated by a regular infusion of ideas and experience from elsewhere. When new recruitment is low, this can be achieved only through secondment and staff exchanges. National schemes are needed whereby academics can change places with colleagues in other institutions or areas of employment for significant periods and obtain professional recognition for doing so.

In many areas of study, especially professional subjects, applied science and technology and the performing arts, it is hard to envisage students receiving an adequate higher education unless they have some contact with teachers whose knowledge is practical as well as theoretical. In less directly practical subjects also, students can learn much that is valuable from those who have practised in politics, administration, industry, commerce, the media and the arts. For this reason if no other, the position of part-time members of staff needs protection, especially at a time when limited budgets make them particularly vulnerable.

In the past a period of full-time academic research has often preceded appointment as a permanent member of the teaching staff of a university or other institution. The funding practices of the research councils are based largely on this assumption. Arrangements are needed which will provide suitable long-term careers for able research workers even if no appropriate teaching posts happen to be available. Research councils should fund a significant number of senior appointments in areas where research is needed but where student demand for courses does not justify a sufficient number of new teaching posts.

IX

THE BINARY SYSTEM

A variety of learning opportunities might be provided by a few large comprehensive universities each covering a wide range of activities and a large catchment area, or by a wider geographic spread of smaller and more differentiated establishments. While the extremes of huge, all-purpose institutions and very specialized monotechnic institutions can easily be rejected, an important strategic choice is whether there should be a move in either direction. On balance, the need to maintain quality and to broaden access in a period of intense competition for resources points in the direction of institutional differentiation. A university or college or polytechnic is likely to have more cohesion if its members share a common perception of its functions. A college that concentrates on providing excellent initial courses for undergraduates should not be judged deficient because it is not doing something else. Furthermore, higher education is likely to be accessible to more students if there is a wider network of institutions.

Any consideration of institutional differentiation must take account of the binary system, which in matters of ownership and control, mechanisms of finance, forms of academic control and salaries and career structures of staff distinguishes universities from other institutions. There are in fact four clearly distinguishable sectors:

i   Self-governing universities.

ii Local authority maintained and assisted institutions.

iii Voluntary colleges, mainly linked with religious organizations and receiving a direct grant from the Department of Education and Science or the Scottish Education Department.

iv Other direct grant institutions.

The institutions at (i), the traditional universities, are on one side of the so-called binary line; those at (ii) and (iii) on the other; some of those at (iv) are on one side and some on the other. Those at (ii), (iii) and the associated part of (iv) constitute what is often known as 'the public sector'. In a number

DIAGRAM 1
Main teaching activities of universities and public sector institutions 1978

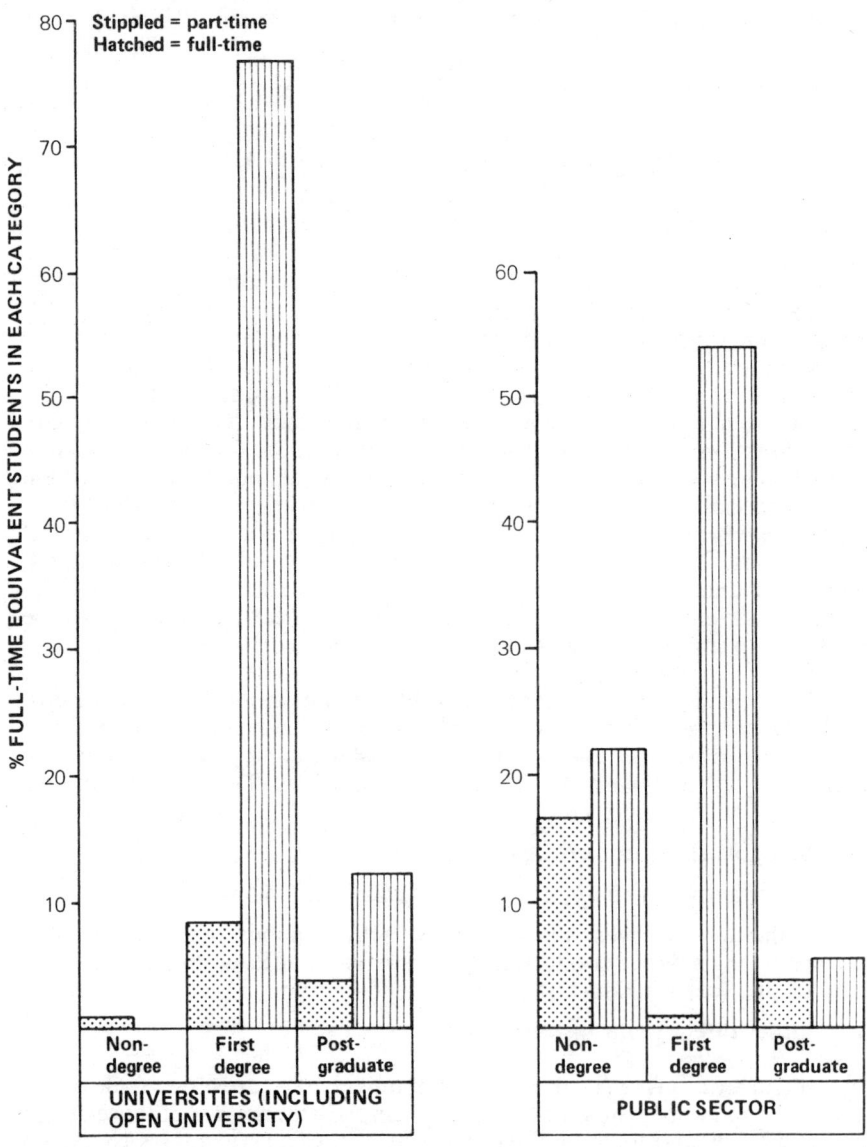

of respects the administrative arrangements for (iii) and (iv) are intermediate between the autonomous universities and the local authority-maintained institutions. Within the public sector there is a further distinction between the institutions (30 polytechnics, 14 Scottish central institutions and 64 other major colleges) with most of their students in higher education courses, and over 300 institutions which have a minority of their students on higher level courses. In very broad terms 60 per cent of full-time students are in the universities and 65 per cent of part-time students are in the public sector (with a further 25 per cent at the Open University).

These administrative differences do not correspond to equally sharp differences in academic outcomes. There are different tendencies, certainly. Medical education occurs in (some) universities only; there is more research in (most) university departments than in corresponding departments in other institutions; there are more part-time students in (many) polytechnics and other colleges than in (most) universities; there is a tendency for most school-leavers to prefer to study in universities, while many mature students seem to prefer public sector institutions. The Open University is a special category, having a Royal Charter yet receiving a direct grant from the DES, and having an academic pattern of courses similar to universities, yet being like many public sector institutions in running mainly part-time courses for mature students. However, as is shown in Diagram 1, there remains a considerable concentration of institutional effort around the first degree in both universities and the public sector.

Does the overlap of academic functions suggest that the binary system should be abandoned? Does the great variety of institutions, particularly in the public sector, suggest it should be drawn in a different place? Should universities and other institutions be more sharply differentiated, with the universities as a group moving more towards the research and postgraduate end of the spectrum while public sector institutions move even more towards sub-degree and part-time work? There are no easy answers to such questions. The binary system involves three distinct differences between sectors: legal and administrative status, mechanisms of finance and methods of academic regulation. It is not clear that the differences in legal status need correspond to the other two distinctions. Similar activities can be performed by institutions with different administrative arrangements. We have suggested that universities should establish some form of organized external academic review in teaching as well as research. This need not damage their status as universities. Conversely there is a good case for appropriate funding to enable at least some polytechnics to develop a significant research capacity and this need not affect their legal position with regard to their local authorities.

More positively, the binary distinction provides what is described in **The Structure and Governance of Higher Education** as a 'moralizing metaphor'. While the role of individual institutions need not be determined by their legal status, the existence of one segment of higher education pulled in the direction of research and scholarship and another pulled in the direction of local and regional social and industrial needs does help to remind members of all academic institutions of the essential diversity of higher education. The binary policy did not prevent drift towards academic courses in the face of demand from students supported by mandatory grants, but it does provide a mechanism whereby different aspects of higher education can be highlighted.

It would certainly be regrettable if the existence of the binary system hampered co-operation between institutions. However, the extent of co-operation between institutions *within* either sector is sufficiently limited to cast doubt on whether it is the distinction between universities and other institutions which inhibits the sharing of resources. The binary system in itself is not an insurmountable obstacle to academic co-operation and joint use of resources and even, in some cases, the merging of institutions. No doubt the blurring of the binary line will continue.

X

THE ROLE OF GOVERNMENT

Central government needs a higher education policy both because of the key role of universities, colleges and polytechnics in the national systems of research, education and training, and because it provides most of the finance. In the fifteen years following the Robbins Report policy was based largely on estimates of student demand. More recent government decisions have been dominated by expenditure-led cash limits. Neither is satisfactory as a basis for policy over the next decade or so. Passive 'Robbins'-type criteria will mean too ready acceptance of relatively low participation rates, arbitrary reductions in activities other than traditional degree courses, and the possibility of an inefficient pattern of provision as institutions compete for a declining number of 'traditional' students. Cash limits not influenced by criteria of educational or social need do not amount to a higher education policy.

Government should have explicit policies with respect to the scale of provision, especially in areas of particular public concern and those which make heavy demands on resources. However, central government should not itself take detailed decisions about individual activities and institutions. There need to be intermediary organizations to advise on the allocation of funds according to the broad policy objectives of government while inhibiting direct political involvement in academic affairs. At present the main such bodies are the University Grants Committee, the National Advisory Body for Local Authority Higher Education (NAB) (and a similar body in Wales), various denominational bodies concerned with the voluntary colleges and the research councils. In Scotland the Tertiary Education Council advises the Secretary of State on issues related to non-university higher education but the allocation of resources is not among the issues which are remitted to it.

The local authority role in England and Wales is considerable and provides an important administrative link between higher education and the rest of the education service. Local authorities reflect local as opposed to national economic and social needs. They are responsible for over 60 institutions whose main concern is higher education and 300 that offer some higher education courses. However, most of the cost of running any particular institution or course is not borne by the maintaining authority itself. Because many of the students come from outside the authority an advanced further education pool was established, to which authorities contribute according to a formula and from which they draw according to the number of places they provide. Until 1979/80 the pool was open and its total size determined essentially by student numbers, which meant that an authority which maintained higher education institutions might meet only a small part of the costs from its own resources. This gave rise to a dilemma which plagued public sector higher education for many years: the ability to commit funds was separated from the need to find most of them. There was increasing central government concern and ultimately the policy of cash-limiting public expenditure led to a 'capping' of the pool. Any local authority spending on higher education above a designated limit must now be met out of that authority's own resources. When combined with the new arrangements for rate support grant under the 1981 Local Government Act the net effect is to give maintaining authorities very firm guidelines on financial allocations to the higher education institutions they maintain.

The role of local authorities is complicated by the wide variety of institutions under their control, ranging from polytechnics, some of which are, by any standards, national and international institutions and have a pattern of students very similar to some universities, to local colleges which provide one or two part-time advanced-level courses in association with their normal work in non-advanced further education. Numerous reports on higher education during the past twenty years have taken the view that while individual maintaining authorities should retain overall responsibility for the good management of institutions under their control, major higher education institutions should have the maximum possible freedom to manage their own affairs. Local authorities need to retain enough residual powers to discharge their legal and financial responsibilities but otherwise they can best involve themselves in the running of institutions through membership of governing bodies.

It is sometimes claimed that some or all of the polytechnics should be taken out of local authority control altogether, on the grounds that they are major higher education institutions which have more in common with the universities than with the rest of the public sector. This was in effect the policy advocated by Robbins and rejected in the 1966 White Paper which established the polytechnic policy. In our view forms of government and mechanisms of finance need not determine academic functions or levels of resources, and the cause of diversity is likely to be best served by a variety of forms of academic government.

Further education colleges with a relatively small number of students on higher level courses raise rather different issues. They demonstrate the impossibility of any clear demarcation between non-advanced and advanced further education. Most of their advanced-level students are not on degree courses and are part-time and therefore locally based. There would be a significant restriction of access for some students, particularly mature students, if these part-time higher education opportunities were no longer available. Proposals for programme funding in Section XI (p.26) are intended in part to deal with this issue.

The National Advisory Body for Local Authority Higher Education was established in England in 1982 for an initial period of three years. Its main task is to advise central and local government on the pattern of provision and the allocation of the available resources in local authority higher education, bringing together national policy and the interests of local authorities which maintain institutions. A similar body has been set up to deal with local authority higher education in Wales and discussions are currently underway for an equivalent body in Scotland where the local authorities have a far smaller stake in higher education. These arrangements have the effect of bringing resource allocation in the local authority sector under a substantial measure of central influence. In effect, agencies have been established which parallel the UGC, taking into account the different administrative circumstances of the two sectors. They provide machinery which will begin to make it possible to devise coherent policies for higher education between universities and the public sector.

Colleges run by voluntary bodies and the other institutions which receive a direct grant from the DES remain outside the direct influence of the NAB. The voluntary colleges are governed by many of the same regulations as the local authority institutions and are subject to similar forms of academic control. We note that discussions are under way which may lead to them coming within the sphere of influence of the NAB. This would help ensure similar treatment of institutions performing similar functions and seems a sensible aim. The remaining direct grant establishments in England account for a very small part of the total resources allocated to higher education and are all institutions which for some reason require special consideration. Their direct relationship with government departments ensures that their resource allocations take into account assumptions similar to those used for other sectors, and there seems little reason for any fundamental change in these arrangements. In Scotland direct grant institutions comprise a large part of non-university higher education and any agency equivalent to the NAB would clearly need to take account of the Scottish central institutions.

The Structure and Governance of Higher Education discusses the possibility of merging the UGC and the NAB into a single funding body. This remains a long-term option, but there are significant differences in the constitutions of the two bodies and of the institutions for which they are responsible. The NAB is recently established and needs time to establish its influence within the local authority sector. Meanwhile the NAB and the UGC should continue the collaboration already started to eliminate obvious anomalies in resource allocation between the main types of courses and subject areas and between geographical regions. It is more important for the UGC and NAB to agree common funding criteria for the many activities that are common to the two sectors than to confront prematurely the difficulties involved in a merger.

Research council funding assumes that research projects in universities will be able to make use of basic facilities and staff financed through the UGC grant. However, the UGC block grant makes no explicit distinction between research and teaching components. Section VII (p.15) has alluded to the danger in a time of declining student numbers that institutional rigidities will result in funds intended for research providing a cushion protecting universities from the need to respond to changing patterns of student demand. The unearmarked research funding received by universities is one of the main sources of the sense of injustice felt by many public sector institutions, both because of the apparent prestige it implies and because of the advantage it gives to the universities in competing for research funds. It is impossible to tell whether similar levels of resources are in fact being provided for similar activities in universities and the local authority sector. Identification of research and teaching budgets would protect research and help to bring about a sharper focus of the national research effort. It would also enable the true costs of different institutions to be seen more clearly.

The funding of continuing education involves some issues essentially similar to the financing of research. It is an activity much broader than higher education, but the contribution of higher education institutions is a key one. In the public sector, in particular, there is a substantial amount of continuing education. Universities have done less and might well do more, particularly in the area of post-experience training and retraining.

Continuing education may need protection if the effects of a declining population of school-leavers combined with institutional rigidities make it difficult for institutions to adapt to new needs. We welcome the initiative of both the UGC and the NAB in setting up working parties to consider its future within higher education.

Like research, continuing education can be funded as an adjunct of the general funding of institutions; it can be funded through a special agency; or it can be funded through the purchase of courses by individuals, firms and government departments. Unlike research, continuing education does not at present have a specialized funding agency: it is provided either out of the general budgets of institutions and local authorities or on a full-cost basis to students or sponsors of students.

The remit of the Advisory Council for Adult and Continuing Education (ACACE) will end later this year. The debate about what succeeds it will involve the role of the Manpower Services Commission (MSC) and local authorities' general educational responsibilities as well as the activities of colleges of non-advanced further education and adult education. A consideration of these issues ranges far beyond the scope of this report. As far as higher education is concerned, the issue is whether present funding mechanisms involving the NAB and the UGC will be adequate to meet the needs for higher level continuing education without a special agency having responsibility for initiatives outside the normal pattern of course provision.

XI

THE INSTITUTIONS

It is in the lecture rooms, laboratories, libraries and workshops of individual institutions that learning and scholarship actually take place. Any external intervention between student and teacher, or between scholar and scholarship, needs to be justified. We have proposed in Section VI (p.13) that one possible justification is the maintenance of standards. Another is the efficient use of public funds in the light of legitimately established national priorities. Universities, colleges and polytechnics are the basic administrative units responsible for allocating resources. They should have the maximum possible discretion in managing their own affairs. Institutional self-government need not mean unrestrained control by academic interests and in practice rarely does. **Agenda for Institutional Change** claims, however, that the separation of academic and non-academic decision-making bodies is too sharp in many institutions and that lay persons are too little involved in critical decisions. Lack of understanding between its main organs of government is not a good basis for the conduct of an organization's affairs, particularly when resources are scarce and the need for adaptation is great. A common criticism of proposals for more lay participation in academic affairs is that it is difficult to recruit competent people who have the time available to play a useful academic role. This difficulty is exacerbated, however, if sympathetic outsiders find they are kept at arm's length from the real academic work of the institutions they are supposed to govern.

Institutions should have a central role in any strategy for the future of higher education but there must be some co-ordination of their separate efforts. Each university, polytechnic and college should have an academic development plan recognized by its main funding body as being consistent with broad national and regional policies. Such plans would be essentially similar to the five-year plans that universities prepared for the UGC before the quinquennial grant system collapsed. Most public sector institutions also have experience of preparing development plans as a basis for claims for resources. However, in a period of adaptation without growth development plans will need to take account of all activities, whereas in the period of expansion it was possible to focus largely on incremental resources and new activities. The need is to adapt procedures rather than create new ones.

Leaders of academic institutions are under pressure from (i) teachers and research workers with professional expertise, (ii) agencies responsible for the implementation of national and local policies, (iii) students, who are the main consumers, and (iv) employers of graduates and users of research. Any mechanism of institutional finance reflects these pressures. It is a compromise. There is a compromise between the claims of academic freedom and the claims of elected governments to establish priorities and require accountability for the use of funds. There is a compromise between the desire of institutions for guaranteed funds to enable them to plan rationally according to their own academic criteria and the wish of external funding bodies to use financial incentives to encourage particular kinds of response. A balance between the pressures can best be achieved, and the independence of institutions safeguarded, if they receive their income explicitly through several different routes.

Each institution whose primary activity is higher education should be entitled to receive core funding in the form of a general grant through the appropriate funding body in accordance with its agreed development plan. Guaranteed core funding can be seen as reflecting the professional interests of members of academic institutions, allowing them to allocate resources according to their institution's own academic priorities. The appropriate level of core funding will vary between institutions depending on their circumstances. The higher the level of its core funding, the more an institution will be dependent on this single source of funds, the less incentive it will have to initiate responses to changing circumstances and the shorter the period for which the core funding will be guaranteed. We consider that over the system as a whole sufficient recognition would be given to the claims of academic autonomy if institutions received on average about half their income in the form of long-term guaranteed core funding. At this level even the most economy-minded government should be able to make long-term guarantees to institutions on the basis of institutional development plans revised every five years or so.

A second component of institutional income should be the full-cost funding of specific teaching and research programmes and projects. This may be seen as reflecting the priorities of bodies responsible for national and local policy. Funding agencies should earmark funds for designated programme areas and institutions involved in the provision of higher education should be entitled to bid for them. As well as being for specific purposes programme grants would differ from core funds in being of shorter duration. There need be no limit on the proportion of their income that institutions could derive from programme grants, but they would be inhibited from relying too heavily on them for fear of over-exposing their financial position. For example, they would be unwise to make academic appointments with lifetime tenure on the basis of programme funds.

Local authorities should be able to give programme grants in both public sector institutions and universities. Some provision for locally-based programme funding could be made in the block rate support grant. Such local authority programme grants might become the dominant form of finance of higher education courses in institutions with a small proportion of advanced-level work. Some funding bodies, for example the research councils, would probably adopt primarily the programme funding mode, while the UGC would probably allocate a relatively small part of its total funds in this way. However, since programme funds would be a powerful instrument for the encouragement of adaptation and innovation, it is desirable that the UGC set aside a significant part of its funds for special programmes. Given the greater variety of provision in the public sector and its greater need to respond quickly to local needs, the NAB and its Welsh and possible Scottish counterparts would probably reserve a larger share of their allocations to the programme funding mode.

The third constituent of the income of institutions should reflect the priorities of student customers. The Robbins Report argued for the maintenance of a significant fee component in the income of institutions. The Committee regretted the decline in the proportion of university income derived from fees, considering it a source of strength that public finance should come through more than one channel, and arguing that up to a point it is better to subsidize students than institutions. Robbins recommended that the level of fees be revised so that they met at least 20 per cent of current institutional expenditure. There remains a good case for student choice influencing but not dominating the orientation of higher education institutions. In the late 1970s home student fees did reach the levels suggested by Robbins, and it is a pity that this policy was subsequently reversed. Individual universities, colleges and polytechnics should be entitled to retain fee income. We assume that home student fees would continue to be subsidized out of public funds.

The fourth source of funds reflects directly the interests of employers and users of research. Income can be earned from full-cost courses and from research, development and consultancy for industrial and commercial enterprises and central and local government. A limited involvement in such income-earning activities will be valuable to many academic staff, broadening their range of experience at a time when mobility will be low. Income can also be earned from the hire of facilities such as buildings, sports amenities and computing facilities. Institutions should be allowed to retain income earned from such sources, although core funding bodies might wish to set an upper limit.

The key element in these proposals is the notion of core funding, guaranteed for long periods but needing to be supplemented to a significant extent from other, less secure sources.[1] If an institution failed to supplement its core income to the necessary extent, the funding body would be obliged to consider whether to reduce the amount of such funds or whether there were good reasons for raising the percentage. Where institutions exceeded their target supplementary income they would be eligible for, but not have an automatic right to, increased core funding.

XII

IMPROVING ACADEMIC LEADERSHIP

Resources and Higher Education draws attention to the need for 'a higher education policy studies institute with an analytical capacity which could

---

[1] In 1979/80 the general component of total income of universities amounted to 63 per cent (see Shattock, M. and Rigby, G. (Eds) (1983) **Resource Allocation in British Universities** SRHE). This corresponds roughly to our concept of core funding. We see it being reduced to about 50 per cent and the difference made good by corresponding increases in the programme funding and student fee components of income.

provide a forum for promoting strategic thinking and planning. undertake independent policy studies and provide institutions and other interested parties with a voice in deciding the principles upon which resource allocation decisions are made.' This proposal arises out of a careful analysis of the difficulty of sustaining any systematic continuing analysis of higher education policy issues either inside or outside government with the present small staff both of the DES and of the main funding bodies and the decentralized arrangements for the management of the system. **The Structure and Governance of Higher Education** comes to a similar conclusion after criticism of the lack of coherence of government policies towards higher education throughout the post-Robbins period. In **The Future of Research** there is a recommendation for the establishment of a forum which would enable producers and users of research to discuss strategic research priorities. A similar case can be made with regard to strategic issues in the education and employment of new graduates.

Adaptation without growth will increase the demands made on leading members of colleges, polytechnics and universities. They will have to respond to new academic developments, new types of students, new technologies and changing demands from labour markets, without additional resources. Professional management expertise. as well as academic ability and innate leadership qualities, will be essential if institutional autonomy and consensus styles of management are to be preserved. **Agenda for Institutional Change** recommends that urgent consideration be given to the type of training needed by institutional leaders, and that provision of such training should be a matter of priority.

Both an awareness of the policy environment and professional management skills will be needed by academic staff who aspire to a significant role in running their institutions. Neither are systematically available across the whole of British higher education at present. We believe that they should be provided and that they should be combined. Active study of the policy environment is an essential prerequisite for high-level professional development. Conversely, the study of policy should be informed by close contact with real problems faced by senior managers.

A centre for higher education management and policy studies should be established with the twin tasks of promoting the study of emergent policy issues and of providing facilities for the professional development of leading members of universities, polytechnics and colleges. The centre need not be a large staff college, and it might be linked to an existing institution. However, the greatest benefit would be derived from a centre spanning both universities and the public sector, and it should be seen to lean towards neither. We would prefer to see an independent centre, possibly linked to an institution not directly concerned with higher education. Its income should come from both sides of the binary line or, which would be preferable in the first instance, take the form of a direct grant from the DES. The essential consideration, especially since its prime aim is to contribute to the conditions in which excellence can be sustained in difficult circumstances in a wide variety of institutions and activities, is that it has facilities and resources to attract high calibre people for short and long periods.

XIII

SUMMARY

THE HIGHER EDUCATION SYSTEM
The higher education system in the United Kingdom is complex. Its activities range from advanced pure research and higher degrees at one end of the spectrum to short practical courses not leading to qualifications at the other. Institutions vary from Oxford and Cambridge, Imperial College and LSE to further education colleges with a single part-time higher education course amongst their programmes of study. Breadth and diversity are sources of strength and should be encouraged.

THE PAST
The decade following the Robbins Report was a period of rapid expansion. The nation's response to the flow of qualified school-leavers appealed to most members of the academic community. The provision of full-time specialist Honours degrees was encouraged with, by world standards, lavish resources, including substantial new buildings and equipment, generous staff/student ratios and mandatory maintenance awards for all students. Most other countries were similarly enlarging the number of students but the British expansion was the envy of many, in terms of the provision of resources and the 'hands off' attitude of British governments.

In the main, the expanding higher education system served the country well. But there were weaknesses. Early specialization in English secondary schools had long been criticized and expansion did little to combat it. The low level of integration of British higher education with industry, commerce and government both in training and research continued to contrast with some of our more successful competitors.

THE FUTURE
The next decade looks very different. In place of expanding demand from qualified school-leavers, the most likely prospect is a 25 per cent fall. In place of improvements in buildings, equipment and staff, universities, polytechnics and colleges are experiencing falling real income and reduced

staff numbers. So far the reaction to this has been largely ad hoc, with no clear strategy. If this continues there is a real danger that the present excellent UK higher education system, which is a great national resource in both productive and cultural terms, will stagnate and decline. With so much that needs to be done, that would be a tragedy. We need a higher education strategy which accords with the circumstances, resources and objectives of the 1980s and tackles the weaknesses which persisted through the Robbins expansion.

This report is not a cut and dried strategy for a sharp change of direction. It does not attempt to lay down a precise new mould into which institutions would be forced. We cannot predict the future in detail. Academic institutions need the capacity to adapt to technological, economic and social change in accordance with the best professional judgements of their members. They should be subject to external influences, particularly through the methods of funding, but not rigid external control.

OVER SPECIALIZATION IN SCHOOLS
This weakness has long been recognized but attempts to redress it have foundered, largely on the rocks of institutional self-interest. These rocks will endure but it is essential for universities to aid circumnavigation by reducing their demands for very specialized entrants. There should be a move to shorter and more general initial courses of study in higher education linked to specialist courses at higher levels.

STANDARDS
The new era will be very much more competitive than the past as universities, colleges and polytechnics struggle to maintain their shares of students and resources. That in itself is not a bad thing. However, it must not lead to a decline in standards of provision. Reviews of performance of institutions, of courses and of members of the academic profession would help to protect quality. Universities should establish an academic review body which should collaborate with the Council for National Academic Awards.

RESEARCH
When resources are generous, research can be supported largely out of general grant money. When the going gets rougher research needs more protection. There should be increased specific funding for research. Universities and polytechnics should formulate explicit research policies for themselves, and these policies should include more emphasis than hitherto on designated research centres. The aim would be a better balance between institutional independence, the protection of research and the orientation of research towards changing economic and social needs.

FUNDING
There should be more institutional differentiation based on the strengths of

individual institutions rather than the type of institutions they happen to be. The study does not recommend the abolition of 'binary' distinctions between universities and the rest of higher education. The number of institutions is so large and the spectrum of their activities so wide and complex that no single funding system can be appropriate to all. But the present differences of approach could with advantage be narrowed and criteria for funding individual institutions made more open. All higher education institutions should have some 'core' funding of a general nature, some grants for specific programmes and some earned income. This would not be a major departure from present arrangements but its explicit recognition would be to emphasize a shift towards a more equitable approach to the funding of institutions and the need to achieve a balance between institutional and professional autonomy, financial accountability for the use of public funds and response to changing social and economic needs.

THE EVOLUTION OF HIGHER EDUCATION POLICY
The next decade promises to be one of the most challenging periods in the history of British higher education. Academic leadership of a very high order will be needed. The necessary response to the challenges needs continuously to be revised, up-dated, monitored and publicized. A centre for the study of higher education management and policy would provide a focus for such analysis and would make a significant contribution to increasing awareness of worthwhile change amongst senior members of universities, polytechnics and colleges.

NOTE OF DISSENT

from Bruce Williams

This note of dissent is the result of differences from my colleagues on three issues.

My disagreement starts with the analysis and recommendations in Section V (p.5). I agree with the judgement that secondary education is too specialized and that there is an over-emphasis on single-subject Honours degrees. But I do not agree that the general introduction of less specialized two-year initial courses, which would give a credential (probably a Pass degree) recognized by employers and those who control entry to subsequent specialized courses, would provide a satisfactory solution (or contribute substantially to greater access). Nor do I accept the suggestion in Section V (p.5) of restricting means-tested mandatory grants for all students to these two-year initial courses, to encourage students to seek, and universities, polytechnics and colleges to provide, courses that could be completed within two years.

Of the five main arguments put forward in Section V (p.8) in support of less specialized two-year initial courses, the first two seem to me to be persuasive only if they are not associated with proposals for two-year degrees. The arguments in (iii) and (iv) that such courses would increase participation rates are doubtful. An increase in participation rates would I think require a substantial increase in specialized initial courses. The argument in (v) that less specialized courses could be provided at lower average cost per student is not therefore persuasive. Developments in educational technology have made it possible to provide a great variety of courses at reasonable cost even in small institutions, by adopting mixed modes of study.

It is ironical that if the proposed change in financial arrangements for student support proved powerful enough to establish two-year general Pass degrees the number of (higher education) students might fall. If the current three-year Honours degree were squeezed into two (longer) academic years, as mooted in Section V (p.10), the number outside the professional faculties would almost certainly fall. The case for such a fall, even at a time when demographic changes are creating major problems, would be strong if standards of performance in Honours degree studies could be maintained. But there is no evidence to support such a change, and the short history of Buckingham, with its limited range of studies and high proportion of mature students, does not provide it.

Because of the depression, and the expected reduction in the number of 18-year-old school-leavers by one-third in the next 12 years, there are strong Treasury pressures to reduce expenditure on education, and doubtless current government interest in two-year degrees has been stimulated by those pressures. But as we recover from the depression and average real incomes increase significantly, Treasury pressures will become less powerful, and community pressures for extensions of education will revive. In the last hundred years, each 10 per cent increase in output per hour was followed by reductions of 3 per cent in hours spent in paid labour. Increased participation rates in education and later ages of entry to the labour force were important aspects of that response to productivity growth, and doubtless will be so in the future. Major changes in education policy should be related to economic trends and not to current fluctuations around trend.

In my view, the case for a multi-sector system is much stronger than implied in Section IX (p.19). The nearest to an exposition of the philosophy of differentiation are the statements on p.21 that the binary system provides a 'moralizing metaphor' and a mechanism whereby different aspects of higher education can be emphasized. There has been a tendency to criticize the binary system on the ground that it is divisive, but far too little attention has been given to the need for institutional differences, and a multi-sector framework of control, to ensure an adequate range of courses, approaches, and educational opportunities.

It is sometimes argued that a multi-sector system permits, even encourages, a movement to the middle ground, and academic drift under the binary system is cited to justify that view. But the Crosland binary system - the multi-sector system really following the creation of polytechnics - did not develop according to plan because the administrative arrangements were defective. Local education authorities were left to sustain and extend 'the kind of education that had its roots in the technical college tradition' without the discipline of programme grants, HND students were not made eligible for mandatory awards, and the charter of the CNAA required it to set 'university standards' for awards.

In Section XI (p.27), it is stated that there must be some co-ordination of the separate efforts of individual institutions and to make this possible each institution must agree with its main funding body a development plan to take account of the whole range of its activities. I do not believe that the UGC could effectively co-ordinate the activities of the relatively small number of universities in this way, and if it attempted to do so it would restrict variety and obstruct the development of new ideas. The problems of co-ordination rise rapidly with scale, and in the public sector the much larger number of institutions would create even greater problems and dangers of bureaucratic blight. 'Broad brush' planning and a rough division of labour between the sectors is the most that should be attempted.

In the pages that follow p.27, there is a move away from reliance on central adminsitration to a more fragmented financial approach, though I suspect that there is still an undue reliance on central administration in the emphasis on the grant of core funding 'in accordance with its agreed development plan'. Oxenstierna's letter to his son contains a relevant warning: 'an nescis, mi fili, quantilla prudentia regitur orbis?'

APPENDIX

A Summary of Evidence

In the programme of study on which this report is based nine specialized volumes have been published:

i   **Higher Education and the Labour Market** edited by Robert Lindley
ii   **Access to Higher Education** edited by Oliver Fulton
iii   **Agenda for Institutional Change** edited by Leslie Wagner
iv   **The Future of Research** edited by Geoffrey Oldham
v   **The Arts and Higher Education** edited by Ken Robinson
vi   **Professionalism and Flexibility for Learning** edited by Donald Bligh
vii   **Accountability or Freedom for Teachers?** edited by Donald Bligh
viii **Resources and Higher Education** edited by Alfred Morris and John Sizer
ix   **The Structure and Governance of Higher Education** edited by Michael Shattock

Each volume contains policy proposals and specially commissioned papers reviewing evidence in the area concerned. The proposals derive from some measure of consensus in specialist seminars, but are *not* agreed recommendations. All have been discussed at specially convened one-day conferences attended by a wide range of interests inside and outside higher education. This Appendix outlines the main issues and policy recommendations that have arisen as the programme has developed and thus provides a summary of the considerations which lie behind the strategy of the report. All references are to articles in one of these volumes unless otherwise stated.

HIGHER EDUCATION AND THE LABOUR MARKET

The British higher education system has never really come to grips with the role it might play in economic development. During the 1980s it must surely do so. This does not mean that the labour market is the only imperative in planning higher education provision. However, that career prospects are very much in the minds of most young people when they seek higher education is clearly shown by the dramatic swing towards vocational studies during the 1970s as the graduate job market deteriorated.

Nevertheless, **Higher Education and the Labour Market** denies the possibility of employment needs providing a simple criterion for higher education provision in the 1980s and 1990s analogous to the Robbins criterion in the 1960s and 1970s. The belief that the labour market might provide a new guiding principle reflects a lack of understanding about the way the labour market works and represents a rather simplistic reaction to the realization that the Robbins principle is no longer a prescription for the continued growth of higher education.

However, in recent years there have been many criticisms from groups outside education, notably employers, of the system's lack of response to the needs of the economy in terms both of satisfying requirements for highly educated manpower and helping to sustain technical progress on a par with that of other countries. Labour market considerations should matter to the higher education system because they provide *part* of the reason why students seek entry and why governments have continued large subsidies. Whether perceptions of the value of higher education depend on the myth or on the reality of the labour market, our universities, polytechnics and other institutions can hardly afford to ignore them. There is, however, a lack of consistency amongst employers who fall into at least as many different interest groups as there are connected with education. It seems doubtful whether there will be a radical autonomous improvement in the responsiveness of *employers* to imbalances in the labour market which might enable the higher education system to play a more supportive role. This makes it difficult to suggest mechanisms that will encourage higher education to respond more sensitively to labour market needs. Higher education may be reorganized to place a premium upon flexibility in course structures, with flexibility given, for example, by modular degrees, opportunity for part-time study or further development of post-experience courses. But if such initiatives are to gather momentum, greater co-operation will be necessary between educational institutions and employers. The book is sceptical as to whether the *supply* of such programmes will materialize without substantial investment in restructuring the system, and whether the *demand* will suffice to warrant the setting up of many of these types of courses without recoupment subsidies to institutions, students or employers.

Governments and employers, as well as educationists, should seek to tackle labour market issues at a more sophisticated level than that reached in the old debate about manpower planning. Labour market evidence does not suggest that higher education has failed industry any more than industry has failed higher education. Educationists need not fear the prospect of regular monitoring on labour market criteria for it is likely to help to clarify issues and, as in the case of scientists and engineers, may sometimes provide a defence against industrial criticism. On the other hand, the outcry of the academic community against crude manpower planning might obscure a general distaste for recognizing the legitimacy of market influences in planning the evolution of the higher education system. Some academics' antipathy towards the labour market may conceal a reluctance to develop and extend the market for educational opportunities. Perhaps a different language, less redolent of the market economy, would help to reconcile higher education to discussing its future structure in terms of its ability to stimulate and satisfy new demands for educational experience.

There is little chance of manpower needs criteria providing a simple guiding principle for the future provision of higher education, but employment needs should influence the size and orientation of a diversified system. There is a need to increase the responsiveness of higher education institutions to the needs of society generally by improving information flows and allowing financial incentives to transmit messages between students, institutions, employers of graduates and government.

Proposals

1 Employers should adjust their employment and salary policies to be consistent with the long-term needs they are articulating.

2 Government should take the initiative in promoting the monitoring of developments in the labour market for highly qualified manpower.

3 Medium and long-term market assessments of likely labour market developments should be made regularly. This would enable potential future difficulties to be assessed, and would lead to a more concerted attempt by both higher education institutions and employers to intervene when problems arose.

4 Courses, at undergraduate, postgraduate and post-experience level, should be more flexible than at present, and should be able to provide supplementary training or retraining for employment.

5 Central funding bodies should encourage the development of the capacity for flexible response, particularly through short, modular courses.

6 The government should consider providing differential grants to students, and should provide incentives for them to develop into areas deemed important for national policy.

7 A greater proportion of the income of institutions should be directly related to their student numbers.

ACCESS TO HIGHER EDUCATION
Access to Higher Education is unashamedly expansionist. Its basic premisses are, that participation in the benefits of higher education is unduly limited and inequitably distributed; that participation will not be substantially increased or redistributed simply by making access easier but only by adapting higher education to meet the needs of an increasingly varied

clientele; and that the forthcoming decline in the 18-year-old population provides an opportunity for major structural change for that purpose without incurring unacceptable increases in expenditure.

Percentages of school-leavers to enter higher education are shown in Table 1. The differences in the trends of the 1960s and the 1970s are dramatic. The participation rate doubled between 1960/1 and 1970/1 and remained static between 1970/1 and 1980/1. The cessation of growth is sharper than that experienced by other Western countries.

The table also shows that fewer women than men have gone into higher education throughout the period. The gap narrowed during the late 1960s and early 1970s but widened again from 1975 to 1980, owing almost certainly to the sharp fall in the number of teacher training places.

TABLE 1
Percentages of 18-year-olds to enter higher education[1] 1960-80

	Total	Men	Women	Women's rate divided by men's rate
1960/1	6.9	—	—	—
1966/7	10.5	11.7	9.2	0.79
1970/1	13.8	15.0	12.5	0.83
1972/3	14.2	15.1	13.2	0.87
1974/5	13.6	14.4	12.8	0.89
1976/7	13.1	14.4	11.7	0.81
1978/9	12.4	14.0	10.6	0.76
1980/1	12.7	14.1	11.2	0.79
1981/2	13.2	14.7	11.7	0.80

[1] As full-time or sandwich students

Source Farrant, J.H. (1981) Trends in admissions. In Fulton, O. (1981) **Access to Higher Education** Table 2.4. SRHE. Later figures supplied by DES.

Differences between social classes are less well documented, but certainly remained greater than those between men and womem. The main effect of the massive expansion of the late 1960s was to improve the relative chances of young people from lower middle-class families - in particular the Registrar-General's Class IIIN, 'Skilled Non-Manual'. These seem to have improved from around 50 per cent of the middle-class average in 1961 to around 80 per cent in 1977. However, the marked difference in participation between young people from 'white collar' and 'blue collar' homes has hardly changed: the chances of working-class children stood at less than 20 per cent of those from the middle-class in 1977[1] (Farrant, Table 2.18). Again, some closing of the gap up to the mid-1970s has been reversed in more recent years. One of the most important revelations of the Robbins Report was that even after standardizing for slightly different distributions of 'ability' (as indicated by test scores), there still remained vast reserves of educationally underdeveloped talent amongst children from working-class homes. Surprisingly, there has been no large-scale attempt to monitor this pool of untapped talent since the time of Robbins. However, Fulton and Gordon[2] have shown that in terms of aspirations and expectations of young people at the end of their compulsory education, the pool of potential intellectual ability that is lost to education at the minimum school-leaving age is as great as it was at the time of Robbins.

Not so widely known are the regional discrepancies in participation. Farrant showed that university participation rates in Scotland are 26 per cent above the England and Wales average, while for the North of England they are 21 per cent below. This discrepancy is all the more remarkable in that, on the basis of the social class mix of the population, very similar participation rates would be predicted in the two regions. There are substantial, though less dramatic, discrepancies in participation rates between other major regions of the country, with Wales, the South-East and North-West of England having higher-than-predicted participation.

Although there are major difficulties in making international comparisons, we can say with confidence that the proportion of school-leavers who achieve minimum entry qualifications for higher education in Britain is low compared with most other Western countries, as is the proportion of 18-year-olds who enter degree-level courses. However, their success rate is much higher than elsewhere, and Britain's production of graduates compares favourably with that of other European countries. In general, British higher education, now as at the time of Robbins, remains an efficient degree-producing machine for a selected minority of school-leavers.

---

[1] Farrant, J.H. (1981) Trends in admissions. In Fulton, O. (1981) **Access to Higher Education** Table 2.18. SRHE

[2] Fulton, O. and Gordon, A. (1979) The British pool of ability: how deep and will cash reduce it? **Educational Studies** 5 (2).

It certainly appears that British higher education has put too much emphasis, both academically and financially, on the full-time Honours degree, and that a greater degree of diversity and flexibility would not only contribute to the future needs of the economy by providing a wider range of qualifications, but also prove attractive to a wider range of potential students; and result both in an expansion in the participation rate and in less unevenly distributed access.

The ability of institutions to respond to new needs has been inhibited by central controls over students' eligibility for grants, over entry standards and over their general institutional development. A greater degree of freedom to create or adapt to new 'markets' would help to achieve the diversity which is needed.

The book proposes that 'all admitting departments should admit at least 25 per cent of their students using criteria other than 'A' levels, including aptitude tests, 'O' level or CSE grades, assessment of prior learning, personal learning contracts, and so on.' There is, of course, a danger that this kind of liberalization would work to the advantage of academically marginal students of the same social mix as at present. The intention of the recommendation is to encourage institutions to recruit from new populations, such as adult students or those who left school at 16, and not to reduce the potential intellectual quality of their intake. If combined with deliberate policies of positive discrimination, it should serve to reduce the actual and perceived inaccessibility of higher education to *socially* marginal students.

The emphasis on the full-time Honours degree has led to an underrating of the possible contribution of alternative arrangements. Even the Open University, so excitingly radical in many respects, had to establish its credentials by allowing its equivalent of an Honours degree to dominate its academic offerings. It is perhaps of some significance that degree courses in Scotland differ in four important respects from those in England. First, students enter the courses in effect one year earlier than in England; second, they decide whether to do an Honours (four-year) or an Ordinary (three-year) degree only after they have been in higher education for at least a year; third, the early years of degree courses are more general than in England; fourth, a much higher proportion of students live at home. These are all factors which make Scottish higher education more accessible, even if they do not by themselves fully account for the higher participation rates.

A diversified pattern of courses and entrance requirements will be complex and will entail a system of credit transfer. This will be hindered by the difficulties of adapting present courses. But an easy first step would be for universities, polytechnics and colleges to issue students with certificates of partial completion (as the Open University already does in effect with its Ordinary degrees and single course units). These could easily become part of the admissions currency for other courses and lead in time to the fuller system of credit tranfer which is clearly desirable.

Financial incentives can encourage flexibility and diversity, and financial mechanisms are the third component in the strategy for increasing access and encouraging diversity. The present grant system might be reorganized so that grants for students in the sixteen to nineteen age group in effect replace those from the third year of degree-level work which could be replaced by a system of loans for further study. It is inequitable that degree-level study, which brings handsome economic benefits in later life, should be heavily subsidized, while full-time education from age sixteen to eighteen appears financially less attractive, not only than paid work, but even than unemployment benefit or its equivalent. A new 'sixteen to twenty' grant might be an 'entitlement', which could be taken at any time and used for any course of education, part-time or full-time, not simply the present full-time degree. The effect would be that potential students could choose from a much wider range of courses, while institutions would be encouraged in return to experiment with alternative modes of study and course lengths. In particular, there would be a powerful incentive for experiments with two-year degrees.

Proposals
1   Courses of higher education should (continue to) be available to all those who are qualified by attainment to pursue them and who wish to do so.

2   It should be the aim of government and of higher education institutions to achieve a substantial increase in the participation rate in higher education.

3   In response to the likely decline in demand from its traditional clientele, the British higher education system should be encouraged to adapt in order to increase participation rates.

4   The same broad principles of response to demand and provision for access should apply to universities, to public sector higher education and to non-advanced further education. The sharp administrative and academic distinction between 'advanced' and 'non-advanced' courses should be abandoned.

5   Courses of higher and further education should be available to all those who can benefit from them and who wish to do so. The 'A' level qualification or its 'equivalent' should therefore continue to be the primary criterion, but all admitting units should admit at least 25 per cent of their students using other criteria, including aptitude tests, 'O' level or CSE grades, assessments of prior learning, and personal 'learning contracts'.

6   The universities and the CNAA should devise certificates of partial completion of degree courses, to be awarded after appropriate assessment.

7   The present grant system should be replaced with a system of 'educational entitlement', whereby every citizen is entitled to support for his or her education or training, regardless of its level. Such support would comprise an age-related maintenance grant and remission or reimbursement of fees, for a maximum of *four* years full-time *or its part-time equivalent* after the compulsory school-leaving age of sixteen. This entitlement should be supplemented with a system of state-supported loans, available for further periods of education or training as desired. It neither precludes nor implies any system of grant support for other courses beyond the four-year minimum (such as postgraduate research or teacher training).

8   *All* institutions, and especially those with highly competitive entry requirements, should undertake significant experiments with positive discrimination in favour of candidates whose circumstances - personal, social or educational - may have prevented them from competing for entry on equal terms with the majority of applicants. When admitted, such students will need special support similar to that given to students entering on 'non-traditional' admissions criteria (such as in Proposal 5 above).

9   It should be the policy of government and of higher education institutions to encourage the participation of adults in courses of further and higher education at all levels, and to make appropriate provision for their special needs.

10 A wide-ranging review should be undertaken, comparable with that by Howard Bowen for the Carnegie Council on Policy Studies in Higher Education (1977), of available evidence on the direct and indirect value of investment in British higher education; where primary research evidence is not available, that too should be undertaken.

11 a   The collection and dissemination of information on demand for and access to higher education should be maintained and where possible enhanced in forms accessible to the widest possible audience.

    b   In particular, the collection of information on access to public sector higher education should be improved at least to a level comparable with that on access to universities, if necessary by specially commissioned research.

c   Documents such as the DES 'Brown' and 'Grey' papers (DES 1978, 1979) and DES **Statistical Bulletin 12/80** are especially useful and should be published at regular intervals as early as practicable. The DES should explore the possibility of providing direct access for qualified specialists to the relevant computer tapes, possible through the SSRC Survey Archive.

AGENDA FOR INSTITUTIONAL CHANGE

Demographic social and economic pressures on higher education during the next decade make change inevitable. Whether it will take the form of decline, or of revival through greater accessibility and responsiveness, depends on the adaptability of the system and those working in it. Four areas of required change can be highlighted: in the relationships between institutions and the wider political system; in the relationships between institutions; in the internal workings of institutions; and in the mechanisms by which change can be facilitated.

Higher Education and the Political System

The relationship between higher education and the state has for many years been relatively uncontroversial. The establishment of the University Grants Committee in 1919 and its development, particularly in the period of rapid expansion in the 1960s, provided a model which was widely considered to be satisfactory. It was designed to ensure, in the words of the Robbins Report, that 'measures of co-ordination and allocation that are necessary are insulated from inappropriate political influences.' Until recently these institutional arrangements were strengthened by two other factors, the availability of resources and the confidence of the higher education community in its ability to withstand political pressure.

While the public sector could not have this conceptually neat model of autonomous institutions protected from political control, the development of the polytechnics was accompanied by the principle of as much separation as possible from political influence. The establishment of the CNAA provided for peer-group supervision of curricula and standards, governing bodies were given strengthened powers and the open pooling system ensured relatively few financial constraints.

This general satisfaction with the relationship between higher education and the political system began to be challenged during the 1970s. The stagnation of student demand and the pressure on resources as a result of the decline in the British economy after 1973 made the arms-length role of political authority no longer tenable. Local authorities began to look more closely at polytechnic budgets to find savings. In the universities the quinquennial system broke down and the UGC began to offer stronger 'guidance' until, in July 1981, it allocated the reduced funds provided by government selectively between institutions and offered detailed guidelines on the area of academic study to which the funds should be applied.

These experiences brought the realization that the political influence of the higher education community had waned. Neither the formal mechanism of UGC and CVCP advice and pressure nor the informal mechanisms of college and clubland dining tables appear to be providing higher education with many friends at court. There are no external constituencies to whom appeal can be made and who are capable of applying electoral or other punishments to those who reduce the resources and the standing of higher education.

In the golden age of the 1960s when students were banging on the doors, and when higher education was thought to be providing economic growth, social mobility and greater equality, there was no obvious need to cultivate a political constituency. It existed naturally. In the harsh climate of more recent years, when students no longer queued and when disillusionment with higher education's contribution to economic and social progress was great, it was too late.

In order to preserve its institutional autonomy higher education has kept those with political power, nationally and locally, at arm's length. This may no longer be possible or desirable. The need to establish or re-establish political links and constituencies is urgent.

The role of local authorities in public sector higher education should not be underestimated. They have the ability to provide independent sources of revenue and to protect their institutions from cuts in government spending. Local authority representatives provide links with the local community and, more importantly, have influence with the education committee. A local councillor who identifies with his polytechnic or college can be a tenacious defender of its interest. There are also advantages in terms of accountability, responsiveness, facilitating links with further education and stimulating the local intellectual and economic environment.

The National Advisory Body for Local Authority Higher Education recognizes the legitimacy of local authority involvement and, whatever more permanent national arrangements finally emerge, should allow for continued local authority participation at both the local and national levels of decision making.

The wider local community should be involved at the institutional level more than at present, through membership of councils or governing bodies. A more radical step would be the involvement of the local community in the strategic planning of each institution. This would be a new departure for many institutions and will no doubt be considered risky by some. If higher education is to regain its political influence it will have to take risks. One of those risks is to expose its inner life to a wider audience. However, allowing people with influence and power within the local community to see what goes on and to identify with the achievements of their local university and polytechnic is more likely than not to increase their support. The notion is outdated that institutions must remain politically neutered to be protected from undue political influence.

National involvement in institutional management is more difficult to envisage but members of parliament ought to be prominent on the governing bodies of higher education institutions with links in their constituencies. This should be part of an attempt to establish a continuous relationship with MPs rather than the more usual situation of only calling upon 'them' at a time of crisis.

What is the appropriate relationship between the central co-ordinating and planning bodies (UGC and the NAB) and institutions? This is more fully discussed in **The Structure and Governance of Higher Education,** but in the context of institutional change the aim must be to ensure that central bodies do not seek to impose uniformity. Instead their objective must be to guide the system towards desirable change and to provide, encourage and maintain diversity in the system in terms of variety of provision and multiplicity of funding sources. Institutions must retain the ability to respond to their own perceptions of the need for change.

In general a greater degree of openness is required. Institutions should be more open to their local communities, and planning and resource organizations should be more open to those affected by their decisions. Without this, the community support necessary to function effectively may not be forthcoming.

Relationships between Institutions
The existence and future of two distinct sectors of higher education has been regularly discussed since the establishment of the polytechnics in 1966. At the level of individual academic activities much co-operation and association exists in professional committees, research organizations and validation bodies. Co-operation also exists and is likely to increase at the course, departmental and institutional level. However this leaves open the question of the formal funding and control relationships between the different institutions. Should there continue to be more than one funding body and if so where should the line be drawn?

For historical, administrative and political reasons two reasonably distinct sectors are likely to remain for some time. However, if the emerging trends continue then the distinction would become less sharp. The proposals made in **Agenda for Institutional Change** are aimed in part at encouraging this trend. Local authorities are likely to continue to have a role in a national body and in relation to their local colleges. If universities offered an enhanced role to local authorities as advocated here and accepted greater external peer review (see below) then in formal terms there would be little to choose between the two sectors. The main distinctions would be that universities through their Royal Charters would continue to have the power to award their own degrees and might continue to receive an element of their research funding through the UGC while local authorities would continue to be able to provide limited additional finance to their institutions.

In the final analysis the form of any structure will be less important than the powers such bodies receive and the discretion they allow individual institutions. Whether the system is unitary, binary or trinary, the structures it creates must encourage initiative, responsiveness, and flexibility so that diversity in provision, access and institutional arrangements can be maintained and fostered.

Credit Transfer
One area in which co-operation between institutions could be improved is in the more ready acceptance by them of students who have completed courses elsewhere. The very least that is required is that a national information service on credit transfer possibilities be established, and the recent announcement by the government of a pilot project in response to the Toyne Report is to be welcomed. More actively, financial levers could be used to push and prod institutions in the right direction. Institutional attitudes might change, for example, if the system for calculating grants were to give an increased weighting to those students who have been accepted through a credit transfer scheme. Skilled use of financial incentives is a powerful way for government to overcome the inertia of academia.

Change within Institutions

The Two-Year Degree The three-year undergraduate degree course is still dominant in most higher education institutions. Proposals for alternative structures usually include the introduction of more two-year courses at diploma level. One difficulty is whether students and employers would accept non-degree courses. As Charles Carter has put it, 'A degree is an ancient and prestigious qualification, and the various diplomas and certificates below degree level carry no equivalent prestige: some are indeed liable to be interpreted as evidence of failure in a degree.'[1]

It is because of this that Cane argues for a two-year degree course linking it to progress for the best graduates on to a two-year Masters course. This proposal has many attractions. It can provide the marketable element which most students are looking for at the end of their studies; it would help to contain costs; as an alternative for those who at the moment take the three-year course, it might attract some students who find present course offerings unattractive; and it would provide a further opportunity for curricular experiments.

---

[1] Carter, C.F.(1979) **Higher Education for the Future** Blackwell.

The objection that degree-level standard could not be reached in two years could be met by lengthening the academic year so that the 90 weeks of study are covered in two years. Staff research and study time could be protected by more generous study leave arrangements as now occurs at the Open University. At the very least some experimentation ought to be encouraged by an enterprising university and by the CNAA.

Peer Review Universities have the authority to grant their own degrees. Polytechnics and colleges require the approval of the CNAA which validates the courses and awards the degrees. The CNAA has been criticized for its bureaucracy and cost and it has recently introduced more flexible procedures, moving towards granting indefinite approval for courses subject to periodic progress reviews.

The key element of the CNAA's approach is the external review of an institution's activity by an academic peer group and it might be timely for universities to ask themselves if they might not benefit from such a procedure. This suggestion in no way challenges their right to award their own degrees. What is suggested is that senates should take advantage of external peer-group review before they grant approval to new courses or renew approval of existing courses. An important aspect of such external review is the self-evaluation which precedes it. The advantages of this are well attested by CNAA and Open University experience. One important long-term benefit might be to raise the status of teaching in universities.

Mobility of Staff and the Principle of Tenure Even with stable financial resources and student demand during the rest of the 1980s the outlook for staffing would be for a gradually ageing academic profession with little infusion of new blood. This is a serious matter, for without the stimulus of fresh thinking and of new aproaches both to research and teaching a higher education institution runs an increased risk of stagnation. When the whole system is involved the situation is magnified. As one contributor to this part of the programme of study put it, 'the worst crime those responsible for higher education could perpetrate over the next 15 years would be to bequeath to the next generation a system in which 80 per cent of the staff was over the age of 45.'

It is difficult to see how mobility can be achieved without an early retirement scheme. Such a scheme should not be devised as a hasty reaction to the need to make economies but as part of a longer-term development in which movement out of the system at an appropriate age might be seen as a natural process and in many respects a sign of career advancement and development. The proposal is not an attack on jobs, but an attempt to substitute some younger academics for some older ones.

The issue of lifetime tenure cannot be avoided. Its importance in defending the freedom of academics from undue pressure and in preventing arbitrary dismissals must be recognized. Yet this importance can be exaggerated. There have been instances where tenure has not been an adequate defence against a strong-minded establishment. Moreover, there are other ways, particularly through the reward and promotion system, whereby unpopular views can be and have been punished. It must be added of course that staff in public sector institutions do not have tenure but are generally covered by normal contracts of employment. There is little evidence that this has inhibited their ability to express their views or to decide their teaching content or research activity.

Mechanisms of Change
The question of how the higher education system can best be induced to produce changes is almost as important as the changes themselves. Higher education institutions do not conform to a single model of organization and decision making, being mixtures of bureaucratic, collegial and market-determined organization. Academic organizations are complex and require able leaders.

Academic credibility is a necessary but not a sufficient condition for academic leadership. It is remarkable that in the universities no systematic training is thought necessary or is provided for those who aspire or are appointed to leadership positions. Polytechnics have the Further Education Staff College at Coombe Lodge but courses are optional rather than mandatory. Prescribing the basis for adequate training is no simple task and is likely to produce heated debate. But it is time at least for the debate to start.

Planning Institutional adaptation and change require effective planning. This should not be conceived in terms of the preparation of grand plans. The purpose of institutional planning is to try to secure an institution's future by anticipating and adjusting to changes in the external environment. In this context planning should be a continuous process in which the effects of old decisions and new situations are continually re-assessed.

Finance Financial arrangements are among the most powerful instruments available to managers of institutions and agencies to influence organization and individual behaviour. Suggestions have already been made as to how finance might encourage change in credit transfer and staff mobility. The principle of giving a larger weight to students whose access funding bodies wish to encourage can be applied to other cases, such as part-time or mature students or those from hitherto disadvantaged groups. These higher weightings could be applied both to the national allocation to institutions and to internal institutional allocations to different departments. More generally the UGC or the NAB might encourage innovation through specific grants. For example, an amount equivalent to, say, 3 per cent of the funds available could be held back and distributed on the basis of open bidding from any institution. It could be granted, for example, for staff development related to new course structures, innovative approaches to teaching, and wider access proposals.

Conclusion
Change within higher education is inevitable over the next decade if only because of demography. If institutions do not react appropriately, change will take the form of an adjustment to decline. Change can also anticipate decline and thus not only prevent it but also bring higher education closer to meeting both the needs of its potential clientele and of the economy and society. It will require courage within the higher education community. Most of the changes advocated here can best (or indeed only) be brought about through decisions within institutions. There are some who believe that institutional leaders have neither the temperament nor the political will for radical change. Time will tell, but the encouraging verdict of those who have studied recent attempts at change in a number of institutions is that learning and adaptation have taken place relatively quickly. It is right to end on the optimistic note that this learning and adaptation will continue apace over the next decade.

Proposals
1 Any new national arrangements for the governance of higher education should allow for an enhanced role for local communities in all institutions in their locality.

2 This role should not only include adequate representation on governing bodies. Consideration should also be given to the establishment by each institution of a strategic planning group with joint lay and academic membership on which local interests would be represented.

3 The local member of parliament should have a seat on the governing body of all higher education institutions within his constituency.

4 The relationship between institutions and their fund-granting bodies should be improved. In particular, institutions should have a voice in deciding the principles on which resource allocation decisions are to be made and any such decisions should be accompanied by a statement of the principles adopted.

5 Any public sector funding body must ensure that it receives information about institutions from a diverse range of sources, including the institutions themselves.

6 While the binary line is likely to remain in formal terms, institutional co-operation across the line should be encouraged, particularly between institutions in the same locality.

7   The recommendation of the Toyne Report for the establishment of a national information credit transfer service should be implemented forthwith. In addition the possibility of using the grant system to encourage institutions to establish credit transfer should be seriously considered.

8   The establishment of a two-year ordinary degree should be considered both by universities and by the CNAA.

9   Universities should consider subjecting their courses to external peer review at regular intervals.

10 A long-term early retirement scheme for academic staff is urgently required. While in the shorter term it might be linked to the substitution of part-time work in the same institution, in the longer term the aim should be to establish a network of links to other organizations which might provide suitable alternative employment. Such a scheme will require extra funds and its establishment is primarily a governmental responsibility.

11 Urgent consideration needs to be given to the type of training required by actual or aspiring institutional leaders. The provision of such training should be a matter of priority.

12 Institutions should adopt an open approach to planning. In the uncertain environment of the 1980s the planning function must take the form of an iterative process in which the effects on the institution of changes in the external environment are continually re-assessed.

13 Instruments of finance and resource allocation should be used as the most effective method of inducing change in higher education.

14 To encourage change, a small proportion of the funds available for higher education (eg 3 per cent) should be open to bidding from individual institutions with proposals for innovation.

THE FUTURE OF RESEARCH
Only 5 per cent of the nation's research and development takes place in institutions of higher education (of this 95 per cent is within the universities). This is a lower percentage of the nation's research and development budget than occurs in most OECD countries, and yet the demands which are put on university research are considerable. There are four principal sets of demands: contributing to the vitality of the nation's research capacity; training the next generation of researchers and improvement of undergraduate teaching; contributing to the solution of social and economic problems; increasing fundamental knowledge, and through this, the attainment of other cultural objectives.

The evidence suggests that British universities and polytechnics are currently failing to meet any of these demands adequately. The reason is not simply shortage of resources. The existing system of funding and management of university research developed during the 1960s at a time of rapidly growing research budgets. Now, with funding for research static or declining, and with even more economic and social demands being made, the system is inadequate. Changes will be necessary.

A central issue is the relationship between teaching and research. The present system for funding university research assumes that the two are closely linked, and allocates research funds on the basis of undergraduate student numbers. The belief in the indivisibility of teaching in higher education and research is one which is held by many academics. There is, however, very little empirical evidence to support the contention, and the surprisingly small number of studies into the subject tend to the conclusion that the links are tenuous, that good teaching at the undergraduate level can be done by individuals and within institutions that do not carry out current research. If this is true and the links between teaching and research can be broken without irreparable damage then alternative methods of funding university research can be advocated. **The Future of Research** argues in favour of a clearer separation of the teaching and research functions of higher education institutions.

However, a more pressing concern at present is the role of the universities in carrying out basic research and contributing to fundamental knowledge which is at risk, given current pressures and resources scarcity. **The Future of Research** recommends that university funding should distinguish between undergraduate teaching and the support of scholarship on the one hand, and postgraduate teaching and research on the other. The UGC should continue to fund both teaching and research but should use different criteria for each. The funding of research would be linked to designated research centres at each institution, and there would be a measure of resonance between general support for research from the UGC and specific project funds provided by the research councils. The recommendation would mean that in consultation with the universities and the research councils the UGC would become more selective in its allocation of research funds.

This method of funding would require each university to have its own research policy and to establish priorities between claims upon its research effort. The policy would determine the balance between fundamental basic research, strategic research, training of postgraduates, scholarship, and research directed to the solution of local, national and international problems. It would identify those departments and units whose past research performance warranted their being singled out for special financial support. Finally, it would help to ensure that new research and people with exceptional research talent had the opportunity to succeed.

A proportion of the total research grant to each institution from the UGC should regularly be available specifically to promote new initiatives identified by the institution. This would help to avoid rewarding with new grants only those which had succeeded in the past; it would enable new ideas to be developed. and young researchers to be encouraged.

At the SRHE Leverhulme seminar on research a few believed that once the split between teaching and research was recognized then the grounds for continuing support of research through the UGC were much weaker. They argued that in such a circumstance it would be more efficient for the funds for basic research to come from the research councils directly. The majority rejected this view on the grounds that it would weaken the autonomy of universities.

It was recognized that it was difficult for universities to make the necessary choices. The development of indicators of research performance might make the task more objective, and hence more acceptable. So, too, would a move to establish a greater parity of esteem for promotion prospects between individuals who excel at the different types of research activity. Although it will be difficult to determine priorities, if the universities do not make these distinctions and formulate priorities, others will do it for them. Part of the price of autonomy is the responsibility for making tough internal decisions.

At the moment, arrangements for determining national research priorities in Britain are inadequate. They cannot be left entirely to the government, with its often narrow and utilitarian point of view. Research workers and users of research should be involved. Higher education institutions, the UGC, the NAB, the research councils, the scientific community and industrial and commercial research organizations should all participate in the establishment of priorities.

Another important theme of **The Future of Research** is the quality of research training. It is suggested that the aims of the PhD should be different from those established by many universities at present. There should be more explicit training in research methodology and more opportunities for research to be done as part of a team. The experience of working for the PhD should encourage flexibility and enable the researcher to move between areas of work within the same discipline. It should be seen more as research training than as a major contribution to knowledge.

The book distinguishes between scholarship and research, especially in the arts and humanities. Scholarship is more closely related to teaching than is research, and the report recommends that the UGC continue to allocate funds to universities for work in the humanities primarily on the basis of undergraduate numbers. Some consider that a research council in the humanities should be established. The evidence was inconclusive. However, it is an important issue and the book recommends that it should be fully explored by a representative group from the universities, the UGC, the Department of Education and Science and the British Academy.

Many of the recommendations made in **The Future of Research** would lead to a concentration of resources for basic and strategic research and to fewer research teams. This, it is claimed, would improve the capacity of the higher education system to meet demands for fundamental research and is essential if British universities are to continue to excel in this respect.

Proposals

1   There should be better systems for collecting statistics on research inputs to universities and polytechnics and these should be devised and implemented by the institutions themselves.

2   More policy research should be carried out to develop indicators of research performance.

3   Each university should have a research policy:

   a   To identify the balance of research effort within that institution which is to be devoted to each of the competing demands on its research system (fundamental basic research, strategic research, postgraduate training, scholarship, and research directed to the solution of local, national and international problems).

   b   To identify those departments and units whose past research performance warrants their being singled out as a centre of excellence deserving special financial support.

   c   To identify mechanisms to ensure that new research, and people with exceptional research talents, have an opportunity to succeed.

4   A forum should be established to enable doers, funders and users of research to participate in the process of identifying fundamental and strategic research priorities in science and technology. These priorities should influence the allocation of resources by the research councils and ultimately by the UGC.

   This forum should enable the views of the scientific community, government and industry to be brought together by a high-level committee with representation from the different interest groups.

5   A similar forum should be set up to suggest priorities for research in the social sciences. It should comprise academics, civil servants and representatives of local authorities and the community at large.

6   There should be a process of consultation between universities, and between the universities and funding bodies, in order to ascertain which institutions will be the designated centres for research in particular disciplines.

7   There should be a new system for funding universities, which distinguishes between the funding of undergraduate teaching and the support of scholarship on the one hand, and postgraduate teaching and research on the other.

8   The UGC should stipulate that up to 10 per cent of the total research grant to each institution should be available to promote new initiatives. The funds should be allocated at the discretion of a research policy group within each institution.

9   A number of social science research groups should be identified as worthy of special support. They should be groups capable of contributing to the solution of critically important policy problems. These selected groups should then qualify for long-term (8 years) support from both the UGC and the research councils. The process of identifying the groups would involve consultation between universities, UGC and research councils.

10 In the humanities, the UGC should continue to allocate funds primarily on the basis of student numbers.

11 The case for a research council in the humanities should be fully explored by a representative group from the universities, the UGC, the DES and the British Academy. The appropriate group to convene such a committee would be the British Academy.

12 The PhD should be seen to be more of a training experience than a major contribution to knowledge. There should be more explicit training in research methodology, and more opportunities for research to be done as part of a team. The experience should encourage flexibility and enable the researcher to move between areas of work within the same discipline.

13 Fees for both undergraduate and postgraduate education should be tax-deductible.

14 The importance of the research function of polytechnics should be recognized, particularly with regard to their contributions to industry. Each polytechnic should encourage the pursuit of research and should have an explicit research policy.

THE ARTS AND HIGHER EDUCATION

Inclusion of the arts as a special theme in the programme was at the request of the Gulbenkian Foundation. and it permitted the examination of curricular issues which would not otherwise have been treated. With the exception of music, the creative and performing arts do not have a long tradition of inclusion in higher education curricula. One point that emerges clearly from **The Arts and Higher Education** is that many of the arts thus defined have close links with particular areas of productive employment and can in no way simply be considered as frills on proper academic or utilitarian curricula. They present serious challenges to conventional modes of teaching, learning and assessment. They all require significant amounts of practical and creative work as part of the process of higher education. Learning to dance, to make music. to perform drama, to compose literature, to create designs, are all of equal importance with the theoretical study of these processes. This presents challenges for course design, for teaching and for assessment.

Other implications which emerged from consideration of the arts include the nature of knowledge. the importance of imagination, and aspects of access that were not dealt with elsewhere. The inclusion of the arts in the higher education curriculum enormously extends the range and nature of knowledge the curriculum can embrace. Traditionally, academic study has been conducted through the written or spoken word, and knowledge has been identified through this process. Many of the arts, however, have to do with a range of knowledge gained and transmitted through the senses, feeling and the emotions. This introduces not only new areas of study and new kinds of assessment, but also adds new and different values for consideration by students and staff. Similarly, the inclusion of the arts gives recognition to the importance of imagination in the process of education and emphasizes a quality which comprises a major part of the wealth of any nation, the imagination of its people. By doing so the higher education system opens its doors impicitly to a range of students previously barred from participation who in Britain have often fallen victim to the vagaries of the discretionary grant system. For all these reasons the creative and performing arts in higher education represent a great enrichment of the system and ultimately of all society.

These arguments present challenges to the dominant position of traditional academic study. In doing so they raise a number of issues which are of direct and logical concern to any examination of the future of higher education. They include changes in the nature and function of the higher education institutions resulting from technological and other changes, with consequent changes in the forms of access and therefore in the student population. Any contemporary inquiry into the future of higher education must contemplate a complete reappraisal of the present system - including its purposes, organization and structures. This must take account of three likely developments:

a   The extension of forms of compulsory education and training up to the age of 18 - with a consequent influence on entry to higher education and a radical broadening of the social class origins of students.

b   The development of continuing education in which the higher education systems will be requied to play a major role through part-time, sandwich, extra-mural and other courses - also with a consequent change in the nature of the student population.

c   Early retirement and the developing concept of a University of the Third Age. The higher education system should extend its traditional concern with young people to include the preparation of older people for alternative careers. for personal enrichment and for new occupations after official retirement at, say, the age of 50. Higher education should also help to equip the entire population for a life in which periods of work are balanced increasingly with periods of non-work.

All this implies a very different style of higher education, with broader purposes and closer links with surrounding communities. This would encourage a stronger role for the arts in the higher education curriculum just as the arts encourage a reappraisal of higher education. Changes in the nature of access and the student body follow automatically. Traditional access needs to be challenged not only in terms of social insensitivity and narrow selection, but in terms of disciplines. Higher education should be opened to a range of artists (and by implication other disciplines) which are now excluded by narrow concepts of knowledge and by an erratic and divisive discretionary grants system.

At the conference which discussed **The Arts and Higher Education** it was emphasized that photography be included with film and television; that combined arts courses are as much 'specialist' courses in their own right as full courses of dance. drama or music, except that they have a different focus; and that seminars of a relatively small number of specialists from the range of disciplines implied by 'the arts' can never do more than initiate the beginnings of dialogue and consultation which needs to be on-going from that point. A regular series of conferences or seminars covering the arts in higher education would go far to clarify philosophy and objectives. co-ordinate methods and raise the status of the disciplines. Such a development would require the initiation of a sound research programme.

The book draws attention to several other issues of general concern which did not emerge clearly elsewhere in the programme of study. Among the most important of these are the links between higher education and the schools. Colleges and universities know little of their students' secondary school work except for the record of examination results. This has the effect of fragmenting the educational experiences of individuals and prejudicing their progressive attainment and development in all areas of the curriculum. 'The broad variety of skills and knowledge which might be cultivated continually over the many years of initial education suffer profoundly through this fundamental lack of liaison.'

One further recommendation has considerable relevance for higher education generally. The part-time teacher should be protected. Just as an expansion of part-time studies is one of the best ways of broadening the accessibility of higher education to students, so an increase in the number of part-time teachers is an important way of opening higher education to influences from outside its walls.

Proposals
1   Urgent consideration should be given to the protection of the part-time teacher in higher education in the arts.

2   There is an urgent need for extensive co-operation across the binary line on a regional and local basis in higher education in the arts.

3   It is important to maintain the diversity of institutions and of courses in higher education in the arts.

4   There is an urgent need for the collection, collation and dissemination of detailed statistics on higher education in the arts and the need for research into questions connected with higher education in the arts.

5   The time has come for redefinition of the appropriate staffing patterns for higher education in the arts.

6   The Calouste Gulbenkian Foundation, the Arts Council of Great Britain, the Crafts Council, and the British Film Institute should discuss together and with others, particularly the Department of Education and Science, the establishment of a research council for the arts and humanities in higher education, adequately funded.

7   The Calouste Gulbenkian Foundation, the Arts Council of Great Britain, the Crafts Council, and the British Film Institute should discuss together and with others the establishment and initial funding of a council for higher education in the arts to carry forward the momentum of the SRHE Leverhulme programme of study:

   i   By encouraging and assisting the formation of action groups for individual art forms, where none exist already.

   ii   By convening a constituent meeting of group representatives to coincide with the launch of the final report of the programme of study.

iii By preparing a plan of work for 1983 derived from the main recommendations of the programme of study leading to a recall conference or seminar in 1984.

LEARNING AND TEACHING

Teaching and learning in higher education has received considerable attention in the period since the Robbins Report. There have been two official reports focusing on university teaching.[1] The Open University has been established, providing new types of courses by new methods of teaching to a relatively new group of students. The growth of new validation bodies, such as the CNAA and the Business and Technician Education Council, has focused the attention of teachers on the hitherto neglected aspects of course design.

Because of the numerous innovations since 1963 the effect of the recommendations of the two SRHE Leverhulme volumes on teaching and learning are not revolutionary, but to many they may appear so because though widely discussed they have not been widely implemented. They are represented schematically in Figure 1.

One of the books' main themes is that there should be more older students in the future and those who are younger should be treated as older. There should be a growth of continuing education and a shift in focus from institutions to students. Higher education systems of the future will need to be adaptable to the needs of students, particularly older students. The growth of continuing education is needed to remedy earlier education disadvantages and because rapid technological development both demands regular updating of skills and creates more leisure. Academic drift has often led to a reduction in the provision and status of part-time and preparatory lower-level work and an excessive concentration on eighteen-plus full-time students.

Part-time study is the key to many essential new developments. Institutions of higher education should be accessible for use by adult students of the surrounding community and types of education traditionally available during the day should also be provided during evenings and weekends. For efficient use of resources this means a re-orientation of full-time courses. Curricula will need to be flexible and the professional development of teachers should include work on the management of older students. Teachers will need to be receptive to new teaching methods and they will need to explore a greater range of acceptable selection criteria including experiential learning credits. This implies a wider acceptance of modular courses and credit transfer combined with local information and advisory services.

---

[1] Brynmor Jones (1965) **Audio-Visual Aids in Higher Scientific Education** HMSO. Hale (1964) **Report of the Committee on University Teaching Methods** (Hale) HMSO.

FIGURE 1

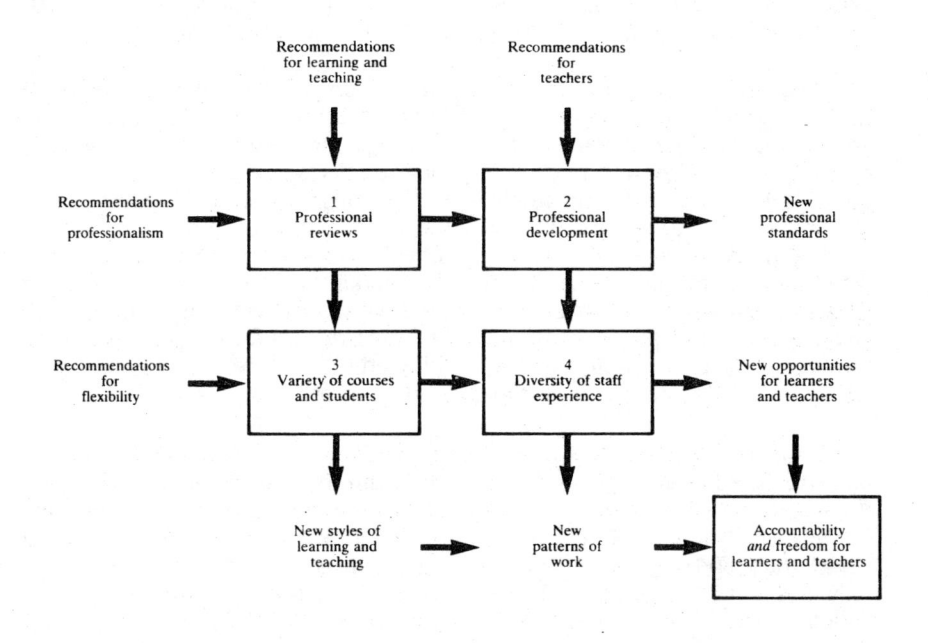

```
                    Recommendations            Recommendations
                    for learning and           for
                    teaching                   teachers
                          │                          │
                          ▼                          ▼
Recommendations       ┌─────────────┐        ┌─────────────┐        New
     for        ───▶  │      1      │  ───▶  │      2      │  ───▶  professional
professionalism       │ Professional│        │ Professional│        standards
                      │   reviews   │        │ development │
                      └─────────────┘        └─────────────┘
                             │                      │
                             ▼                      ▼
Recommendations       ┌─────────────┐        ┌─────────────┐        New opportunities
     for        ───▶  │      3      │  ───▶  │      4      │  ───▶  for learners
  flexibility         │ Variety of  │        │ Diversity of│        and teachers
                      │  courses    │        │    staff    │
                      │and students │        │ experience  │
                      └─────────────┘        └─────────────┘
                             │                      │                      │
                             ▼                      ▼                      ▼
                      New styles of            New                  ┌─────────────┐
                      learning and   ───▶   patterns of  ───▶       │Accountability│
                        teaching              work                  │ and freedom for│
                                                                    │learners and teachers│
                                                                    └─────────────┘
```

The changing composition of the student body will require a style of higher education that is consultative, considerate and flexible. Staff will need to be aware of the effect of their teaching on their students and be sensitive to the factors which inhibit good relationships with them. Students need personal feedback on their performance. There should be professional development units. Institutions should encourage faculty boards and academic departments to appoint or designate specialists who have a special interest in the study of the teaching and learning of their subjects. These double specialists will work with their colleagues on the design and management of courses. Professional development units should concentrate upon the education and training of such specialists and, in collaboration with these specialists, upon the professional induction and development of new staff. This is not to say that these should be the only duties of professional development units. They have important roles in the dissemination of new ideas on teaching and learning, in liaising with other institutions, in developing the art of professional development, in the conduct of inquiries and research both within their institutions and outside them, and in the general promotion of new standards of teaching by discussion and co-ordination of professional development work within their institutions.

The difficulties in implementing professional development plans need to be recognized at a senior level within institutions. Departmental groups are, by their nature, often resistant to change. Professional development is easily perceived as a threat to an individual's self-esteem. There is an inadequate basis of knowledge for professional development and development of teaching will be difficult while incentives seem to favour the development of research. There is need to institutionalize professional development and institutions will need to make explicit policies for it. Such policies will need to include regular reviews of the aims and career development of staff. There should be systematic and formal procedures for the evaluation of teaching and there will need to be some policies relating to the special needs of heads of departments and other senior staff.

Some of the more sensitive aspects of professional development cannot be established by a single institution, or within it, and this indicates a need for some co-ordination of professional development between institutions. Sharing of experience across the binary line, at present fairly limited, would be to the good of all. A national organization to promote professional development could act as a clearing house for the provision of specialists, it could assist the development of skills in professional development itself, it could keep the evaluation of professional development under review, it could promote national policies and be a national focus for consensus on professional development issues. However, it is not recommended that there should be an elaborate and bureaucratic institution with a large number of permanent staff.

Another example of the need for central initiative is in the area of encouraging staff mobility. Institutions should take steps to maintain and increase:

a   The mobility of staff by industrial, commercial and professional transfers, secondment and exchanges.

b   Study leave.

c   The use of part-time and temporary staff.

However, individual institutions will be unlikely to achieve these goals on their own. Some central encouragement and co-ordination will be required.

All recommendations to improve professional standards and to create new opportunities for learners and teachers will be ineffective if there is no mechanism to evaluate professional standards and to assess the new opportunities that are offered. Professional peer reviews are the mechanism, consonant with academic freedom, to implement the proposals set out below. Professional peer reviews involve no new principle. Indeed many institutions claim that they are common and regular practice. However, the processes themselves should become more systematic and open. There is a need to evaluate the curricula in terms of the needs they satisfy, the aims they achieve, their content, their methods and their balance between theory and practice and between the needs of both society and the individual. Institutional reviews of their assessment procedures for students should examine *with* students (a) the relationship of assessments to curricular aims, (b) the variety and reliability of assessment methods used, (c) the methods of communicating results, and (d) the grading system adopted. The educational processes of higher education should become subject to the processes of free critical inquiry that are the basis of higher education itself.

Proposals
1 Institutions of higher education should ensure that the design of courses and the processes of teaching, learning and assessment are more open than they are at present, and are subject to regular peer reviews.

2 Particularly in vocational subjects or fields, curricula should be developed after discussions with professional associations or other relevant organizations.

3 There should be an ombudsman whose judgement might be sought of the quality of teaching.

4 New standards of professional competence need to be established, and this includes competence in peer reviews as well.

5 While recognizing that curricula in higher education must reflect the content, methods and inner logic of the disciplines being studied, teachers should ensure that they neglect neither practice nor theory, and that they take account of the needs of both society and the individual.

6 Courses should be manifestly student-centred.

7 Teachers in higher education should explain clearly to students the aims, structure, procedures, requirements and methods of assessment (if relevant) of their courses.

8 Teachers should help students to take maximum responsibility for their own learning.

9   Courses should be designed to focus upon the tasks through which students will acquire and display excellence of both mind and practical skills, rather than upon the exposition of a series of topics by teachers.

10   Styles of teaching should be developed such that working relationships between teachers and students are valued by both.

11   Institutional reviews of their assessment procedures for students should examine:

   a   The relationship of assessments to curricular aims.

   b   The variety and reliability of assessment methods used.

   c   The methods of communicating results.

   d   The grading system adopted.

12   Institutions should encourage faculty boards, and academic departments should appoint or designate staff, to have special expertise in the study of the teaching and learning of their subject. In collaboration with their colleagues, these specialists will exercise responsibilities for course design and course management.

13   Professional development units should concentrate upon the education and training of such specialists and, in collaboration with the specialists, upon the professional induction and development of new staff.

14   While maintaining academic standards, institutions and validating bodies should encourage more flexible patterns of, and access to, courses for individuals in higher education.

15   A feasibility study should inquire how far it is possible to assess experiental learning for entry to or exemption from specific courses.

16   A study should investigate the feasibility of providing more opportunities for students (on payment of fees) to be assessed for higher education qualifications without having taken a specific route to prepare for the assessment.

17   A working party should be set up to study the feasibility and desirability of new patterns of degree courses.

18   Institutions in higher education should be prepared to place much more emphasis upon the needs of older students.

19   Institutions should take steps to maintain and increase:

   a   The mobility of staff by industrial, commercial and professional tranfers, secondments and exchange.

   b   Study leave.

   c   The use of part-time and temporary staff.

RESOURCE ALLOCATION IN HIGHER EDUCATION

In future, higher education will have to compete more fiercely for resources against other sectors of education and other types of public expenditure. Its vulnerability is increasing as numbers in the 18-25 age group start to fall. Public expenditure on higher education will depend not only upon the political outlook of future governments, but also upon the ability of the Department of Education and Science to develop and pursue its case with the Treasury. The success of the spending Minister in obtaining the funds necessary for his policies depends not only on his negotiating skill and political standing, but also on the effectiveness of his Department's support and the political importance of his policies. The case for higher education will be more effectively made if the Secretary for State for Education and Science formulates long-term policies for higher education and negotiates with the Treasury within the framework of these policies. This is preferable to disjointed decrementalism.

How should policies and strategies be formulated, given that the ability of the DES to conduct major policy studies is limited by their relatively small numbers and lack of experience within the higher education system? The DES should have access to an analytical competence in policy analysis, but this competence need not be located wholly or even chiefly within the Department. Furthermore the policy formulation process should be a two-way one, with the DES and other government departments issuing scenario analyses and discussion documents and listening not only to responses from the NAB, UGC, CVCP, CDP and other interested parties, but also receiving their, and other independent analyses and proposals.

Grants, Fees, Student Awards, Loans and the Market Mechanism
Resources and Higher Education reports divided opinions on whether greater flexibility should be introduced into the student support system through a combination of grants, loans and fees, so as to move 'voting power' towards the students in a manner which would be consistent with institutions becoming more market orientated. A central issue in the debate is whether the market mechanism should be used to reduce the number of institutions as demographic trends bite, or whether the advice and decisions of the NAB and UGC would result in better resource allocation. Given the rigidities in the system, one view is that market mechanisms might create unmanageable financial pressures and uncertainties for all institutions. Once

a market in higher education had been created it would have to be controlled. An alternative argument is that adaptable, flexible and efficient institutions would respond to the incentives structure created and would prosper whilst less efficient institutions would need to adapt or risk being eliminated.

Opinions are particularly sharply divided on whether there should be a change in current fee levels: those who advocate higher fees recognize that they would have to be accompanied by institutional resource allocation procedures that stimulate flexibility and adaptability.

The book reports substantial agreement that a system of financial support to students that combined loans and grants would be more flexible and adaptable than the present reliance on grants alone. If governments would allow a re-distribution within higher education of loan repayments, it would in the long run release scarce resources to support the widening of access, part-time courses, continuing education, and emerging priority areas.

Funding Mechanisms in the Public Sector
Public sector institutions offer advanced and non-advanced-level courses to meet national, regional and local needs, attracting both full-time and part-time school-leavers and more mature students on degree and diploma courses, while also offering a wide variety of professional and short courses. Given this diversity of activity, the sound financial management of polytechnics and colleges must be able to rely upon some guaranteed funding for those 'core' activities which cannot quickly be modified in the short run. Without one or two secure sources of finance it is doubtful whether institutions can be effectively managed, but the proportion of income from 'core' funding should not be so high as to discourage entrepreneurial initiative at a time when institutions should be seeking a higher proportion of their funds from non-public sources.

Polytechnics and other 'major' institutions should look to the NAB for the determination of their 'core' funding for first degree and sub-degree courses, and part of the national pool should be available to local authorities to provide funds to meet specific local and regional needs. Local authorities could also fund specific activities on a customer/contractor basis. It can be argued that a movement towards higher fees and market mechanisms would add additional, and possibly unmanageable, uncertainties to an already 'messy' and complex situation.

The NAB should call for, respond to, and co-ordinate plans and proposals initiated within institutions themselves. Whilst inter-institutional cost comparisons should provide a starting point for 'value' judgements incorporating, whenever possible, quantitive and outcome measures, they should not in themselves determine the basis of resource allocation by the NAB.

There is also the question of the relationships between the NAB and the UGC, which embody the two sides of the binary line. Given the complexities of the public sector, any talk of a merger would be premature. It is desirable that the NAB should be given time to become well established, and the NAB and the UGC should develop effective liaison and co-operation before thoughts of a single higher education grants committee are pursued.

Funding Universities
A number of models for the future financing of universities can be envisaged, ranging from variants of the old quinquennial system to ways in which more private money can be injected, combined with greater market freedom for the universities. The role of the UGC would vary significantly between the models. Any discussion must confront the inflexibilities and rigidities in the current staffing situation, as regards both the age and distribution of staff and the nature of tenure in some universities.

There is widespread scepticism whether self-governing institutions are capable of managing contraction, adaptation and change, in response to market forces. There would be resistance to closing departments, squeezing existing activities to create innovation funds, and developing and implementing a strategy to cope with the bulge in the age distribution of staff and to ensure there is a constant flow of new, young blood. Redundancy and retirement must be an important part of the adjustment process, and if it were left to institutions they might not make decisions in the long-term interest. Such considerations point to a positive role for the UGC in stimulating institutions to develop plans for their future development, in providing guidance, and co-ordinating the overall contraction, adaptation and change of the system, whilst at the same time preserving reasonable institutional autonomy and stimulating entrepreneurial activity. The UGC should liaise with the NAB to ensure that the higher education system as a whole is responsive to national needs and priorities.

Doubts are expressed about radical, market orientated models of universities: it is preferable to adapt a proven and widely respected UGC 'core' grant model. The dirigiste UGC devil we know is preferred to the market mechanisms devil we do not know.

Consideration is given to the question of research funding. Should the UGC continue to provide a single block grant for teaching, scholarship and research, should it give a separate grant for research, or might more money be given to the research councils, with the UGC concentrating upon funding teaching and scholarship? It is essential to protect research capacity in universities and to maintain a diversity of sources of funding for research. The UGC should provide separate research grants, with specific guidance to universities in response to institutional plans and proposals, and no more resources should be moved to the research councils. Given that fundamental research is also undertaken in a number of public sector institutions, a corresponding approach to research funding might be appropriate for that sector.

Institutional Research Allocation
Declining student numbers and falling real income per student have their sharpest impact at the institutional coal face, where limited resources are actually transformed into educational services. The major managerial challenge will be to maintain institutional vitality, creativity and responsiveness to changing needs when all the pressures may well be working in the opposite direction. The aim must be to manage not just for survival but for excellence, and resource allocation processes should be consistent with this objective.

Current pressures on institutions are highlighted by the book, and the need to be able to return to real planning is emphasized. While in periods of expansion decentralized resource allocation processes are appropriate, in decline there is a strong case for greater central control. In particular, institutions need to maintain a central innovation fund.

There is some scepticism about rigid and detailed academic plans. Institutions have to get used to uncertainty. However, the greater the uncertainty the greater the need to develop strategies and long-term plans to cope with it. The performance assessment and organizational and behavioural aspects of the planning process are critical. Planning has to be a participative, interactive process, with positive leadership from the centre. Institutions need to develop strategies for long-term resource mobility as well as for short-term survival. Agreed long-term strategies need to be translated into detailed action plans for academic departments and units, which define not only the role of the department but also the appropriate measures of performance.

In the absence of well developed plans, there is a danger of marginal resource allocation decisions which are not consistent with maintaining the longer-term vitality, responsiveness and creativity of the institution. Thus, decision-makers within institutions must ask themselves whether their resource allocation formulae are compatible with their long-term objectives and strategies.

In managing institutional contraction university councils and the governing bodies of public sector institutions have to play a stronger role than in the past. The planning process has to involve the academics in the operating units, but in the end many institutional resource decisions will have to be centrally determined.

Innovations in response to new needs and new opportunities frequently occur through the initiative of individuals. Directors, principals and vice-chancellors of institutions will have to create an environment which motivates individuals and fosters such initiatives. Not only should they support staff of high ability but the performance of all staff should be reviewed regularly with a view to increasing their effectiveness. A central innovation fund within each institution is needed, and institutions must, in their own interests, seek to protect their centres of excellence. Fair shares for all will not work in the long run.

In order to stimulate entrepreneurial activity and reduce reliance on public funding, an appropriate structure of incentives and rewards should be created. It is equally important to control the balance between academic and entrepreneurial activity; to exercise proper financial and managerial control over such activity; and to ensure that the desire to maximize personal and department income does not dominate the academic roles of departments.

Resource Allocation and the Binary Line
It remains a matter of contention whether all institutions whose primary activity is teaching full-time undergraduates drawn from a national pool of applicants should make their case for 'core' finance to a single source. The binary line may be imperfectly drawn, but for resource allocation purposes it exists and has a rationale: it separates a research-led sector, funded through the dual support system and having a broadly national perspective, from a sector with a local and regional perspective which either is or could be led by the patterns and policies of schools and further education colleges. This supports the case for local authority influence - though not necessarily control - over a schools and further education-led cluster of higher education colleges and polytechnics. Nevertheless a unitary rather than binary system may be one of the consequences of the view which favours the determination of rationalization and contraction not by market mechanisms but by grant awarding bodies. If full-time undergraduate numbers were to fall by 30 per cent between 1981/2 and 1995/6 the government would need to form a view as to how this contraction should be handled either side of the binary line. The use by the NAB and the UGC of the dirigiste scalpel will necessitate close collaboration on both national and regional rationalization but may create tensions. These may lead the government to the view that a single source of funding is essential, but the many other actors on the higher education stage may not agree, and it may not prove possible for the DES to establish a consensus in favour of change, or to ensure that legislative time is made available.

Conclusion
Overall, conditions of contraction, financial stringency and changing needs require a 'top down' DES/UGC/NAB statement of policies, objectives and guidelines, 'bottom up' responses from institutions, advice to the DES from the NAB and the UGC, and 'top down' DES/UGC/NAB decisions. Following agreement of plans with their funding bodies, institutions would have to ensure their resource allocation procedures were consistent with their corporate plans and with those of their departments.

Proposals

1 The government should establish and enunciate broad policies, strategies and guidelines for the higher education system, including guidance to the NAB and similar bodies and to the UGC on the considerations to be taken into account when making decisions and recommendations to Ministers concerning institutions, student numbers, subject areas, courses and allocation of resources to institutions, or to the research councils concerning research priorities and establishment of centres of excellence.

2 The DES should seek private and public funding for the establishment of a higher education policy studies institute with an analytical capacity, which could provide a forum for promoting strategic thinking and planning, undertake independent policy studies, and provide institutions and other interested parties with a voice in deciding the principles upon which resource allocation decisions are made.

3 Financial support to students should be by means of a combination of loans and grants.

4 Whilst public sector institutions should continue to satisfy a variety of needs and attract finance from a large number of sources, it is essential for the financial stability of institutions that core funding should be provided from one or two sources. The NAB and similar Irish, Welsh and Scottish bodies should call for, and respond to, plans and proposals from institutions and recommend allocations of 'core' block funds (being the larger part of the funds nationally available) for first degree and sub-degree courses, after evaluating proposals in the context of national and regional frameworks. The LEAs should allocate a smaller part of the funds nationally available for individual authorities to fund initiatives either side of the binary line. In addition, LEAs should undertake from their own funds specific funding on a customer-contractor relationship, as well as 'topping up' with grants from their own funds if they so wish. Given the multiplicity and complexity of sources of funding, it is essential that institutions have a strong financial administration with sound resource allocation and financial control systems. Institutions should have greater freedom to vire between heads of expenditure without seeking the approval of the maintaining local authority.

5 The UGC should collaborate closely with the NAB. They should respond to plans and proposals from institutions and continue to provide selective guidance based on judgements of the relative merits of departments and subject areas. They should provide separate block grants for teaching and scholarship and for research. The funding of research should not be linked directly to undergraduate numbers.

There should be a multiplicity of sources of research funding, and specific funding should continue to be provided by the research councils. Both the UGC and the NAB should maintain a central fund to finance new developments and innovations and to facilitate adaptation and change in the system. They should encourage efforts to increase funding from non-government sources and facilitate entrepreneurial initiatives.

6 Institutions should recognize that under conditions of contraction, declining resources and changing needs, planning and resource allocation need to be more centralized. They should ensure that there is nevertheless extensive consultation with academic departments and units. Each institution should:

a Develop a strategic plan which includes a strategy for survival (short-term) and resource mobility (long-term), and provide mission statements for each academic department and unit.
b Ensure that its resource allocation procedures are consistent with the strategic plan and mission statements.
c Establish a separate university research budget and identify those departments and units whose past research performance and future potential warrants their receiving preferential treatment.
d Establish a central innovation fund to support new course and research initiatives and to develop staff of outstanding teaching and research potential.
e Seek to increase the share of funding from non-governmental sources, and introduce appropriate incentives to foster entrepreneurial activity, whilst ensuring that such activity is consistent with the teaching and research missions of departments and with the appropriate financial rules and procedures of the institution.
f Recognize that contraction and adaptation will require fewer, high-quality administrative staff.

7 Salary scales should continue to be negotiated nationally. Employers' representatives in negotiations on salary and conditions of service should:

a Recognize the need to facilitate and not inhibit institutional vitality, adaptation and change.
b Ensure the maintenance of maximum flexibility so as to encourage staff mobility, and to allow a regular flow of able young teaching and research staff to be recruited with reasonable career prospects.
c Recognize that long salary scales are incompatible with stimulating institutional vitality.
d Ensure that early retirement schemes are available.

STRUCTURE AND GOVERNANCE

In October 1963, when Robbins reported, higher education seemed set fair to develop on a clearly marked out track. Expansion would take place largely in the universities. Their near monopoly of degree-level work would be reinforced by the upgrading of the colleges of advanced technology, the development of functional links between universities and the teacher training colleges and the creation of five new technological institutions. A single grants commission would be responsible for advising government, through a new minister for arts and science, on the needs of all autonomous institutions of higher education. This tidy world was not to be. The government did not agree to the functional linking of the colleges with the universities, did not create the new technological institutions, did not reform the UGC, and moved responsibility for the universities over to the Ministry of Education. Since then it has created the polytechnics and a public sector of higher education, cut off many universities' relationships with the (re-named) colleges of education and merged many of the colleges into the polytechnics. Most recently, it has established the NAB, a parallel body to the UGC, with a minister in the chair, to advise on co-ordination of the public sector.

The Structure and Governance of Higher Education is concerned largely with the question of whether the system which has evolved since Robbins is adequate to meet the needs of the country in the 1980s and 1990s. Changes have occurred piecemeal, and inadequately planned administrative solutions have often taken precedence over the educational or social; unnecessary controls are cramping individual and institutional initiative. There has been inadequate consideration of the various policy options available and there is need for a new forum, outside the DES, where higher education policy can be researched and discussed.

The first problem needing solution relates to the relationships between institutions and the public perception of the structure of higher education. Historically there has been a tendency in Britain to see higher education in terms of a hierarchy of institutions and to allot status to types of institutions without defining whether that status derives from academic quality, funding or social prestige. The establishment of the polytechnics by Crosland in 1965 and the enunciation of the principle of the binary line introduced a further element into the hierarchy. Neither sector of higher education, however, is homogeneous and the differences, for example, between Oxbridge and the technological universities or between the polytechnics and the voluntary colleges are in many ways at least as marked as the binary line itself. The creation of the NAB as a parallel body to the UGC has, however, brought the binary division into sharper focus. The new body may in time improve the planning of the public sector and enable better co-ordination to take place between the two sectors, both functions being particularly important in a period of retrenchment, but it also has the effect of further institutionalizing a division in higher education which, almost inevitably in the British context, exacerbates the establishment of a rigid academic and social pecking order.

The concept of a hierarchy of institutions and divisions based essentially on administrative arrangements should be replaced by a more egalitarian system where institutions are distinguished primarily by function. Burton Clark makes the point in his contribution to the book that 'Institutional integrity has been weakened in many national systems during the 1960s and 1970s, first by greater governmental involvement attendant upon expansion and then from top down efforts to contract and consolidate.' A first step to achieving a more egalitarian system must be for the government and the funding agencies to give more emphasis to institutional autonomy, particularly in the public sector, and more encouragement to institutional initiative. This would not only push planning and decision making down more firmly to the institutional level but would stimulate greater diversity amongst institutions. One of the worst features of our present ranking of institutions is that it encourages 'academic drift' and a greater homogeneity of approach, whereas higher education would be strengthened by more institutional individuality. Diversity should be reinforced by the provision of multiple sources of funding and greater institutional responsiveness to national, regional and local needs. In addition, and as a prime central planning tool, institutional 'mission statements' should be established, after discussion between the institution and the funding agency, thus linking institutional function and purpose with funding. This emphasis on diversity of institution and institutional initiative needs active encouragement. One important result would be a strengthening of institutional self-government mechanisms and a withering away of the significance of the binary line.

One of the continuing debates about higher education governance relates to centralization. In the past the UGC has centralized resource allocation decisions on the university side, but the public sector institutions have been subject to more detailed financial and academic national, local and regional controls. The creation of the NAB might seem to lead the long march towards the centralization of all decision making about higher education. In practice the NAB has laid great stress on the involvement of the regional advisory councils, and this should be encouraged. Higher education, however, needs strong central mechanisms and while there should be a continuing local authority involvement in the governance of higher education both at institutional level, through governing bodies, and at national level, some transfer of strategic planning to the centre is both desirable and inevitable. An emphasis on institutional autonomy and initiative would be an important factor in ensuring that local interests continue to play a significant role in higher education decision making. Much more effort should be put into local and regional co-operation between institutions and the first step should be voluntary machinery established between the institutions themselves. Further collaboration might be encouraged by financial incentives from UGC and NAB. The whole area of adult and continuing education provides a particularly important focus for local and regional co-operation, and representative local committees should be set up to bring together institutions, local authorities and other providers.

The implementation of the 1981 expenditure cuts brought inevitable criticism of the UGC and claims of lack of accountability. The UGC should not be turned into a representative body but the time has come for it to become a more open body, and to publish its criteria for decision making. The staffing of both NAB and UGC has also become a matter of concern. Comparisons with US state higher education co-ordinating agencies suggest that, while in the past the UGC has had exceptional success in maintaining the respect and trust of the universities and the government, the pressures of contraction and financial stringency will place very great demands on high quality staff work, an area where the UGC suffers when compared with the US agencies. As long as staff are recruited only from the DES mistrust by the universities is likely to persist. The situation might be improved if both UGC and NAB were able to bring in a substantial number of staff seconded from higher education.

Increasingly, as higher education takes on greater responsibilities in the fields of research and training in areas of national economic importance, its location under the DES umbrella becomes less plausible. It is clear that a number of other government departments are keen to play a larger role in higher education and have a substantial stake in the higher education process. This applies to departments with specific interests like DHSS and Agriculture and to one like Industry whose interests and research funding have a major impact on scientific and technological development. The role of the DES must of course remain paramount, but for the long-term future of higher education it is essential that a better interface be created between institutions and relevant government departments, and that government should find a way of recognizing explicitly the part that higher education can play in economic recovery. Higher education has a significant role both in training and research, helping to convert Britain from its present acceptance of economic decline, but new mechanisms need to be created whereby higher education can respond more quickly to external demand and in some fields can be better integrated into government programmes of research and development.

The creation of the NAB represents the culmination of a long process of attempts to achieve better co-ordination in the public sector and it is crucial that UGC, NAB, their subject committees and their secretariats embark on a close and systematic process of collaboration to ensure that a proper planning machinery is devised for higher education as a whole. The NAB has a three-year brief, but it is inevitable that its life will be extended in some form. In the longer term the continuance of the two bodies working under separate remits raises very important questions. Some argue that the two sectors should remain separate and that the two bodies should be subordinated to an overarching body whose function would be to plan the whole of higher education. Others claim that the natural development would be to bring UGC and NAB together, with the added benefit of removing over time the administrative frontiers created by the binary line. This is strengthened by the belief that the creation of a third co-ordinating body could not be justified in the present economic climate, and would present such difficulties of assimilation between the legitimate powers of the Secretary of State and the existing UGC and NAB that it is unlikely that it would ever become an effective agency. A contrary view, however, is that the Secretary of State needs advice independent of the recurrent grant awarding body and that an overarching advisory body is required, leaving the powers of the UGC and the NAB intact. This latter view looks increasingly unrealistic in present conditions.

Tied in with discussions about governance are questions relating to validation and the course control mechanisms operated by the DES. In particular, the relationship of CNAA to NAB and to universities raises significant issues. Should CNAA become an academic arm of NAB, or should university degrees be brought under CNAA procedures? Is it right that polytechnics and other institutions of higher education in the public sector should be subject to such heavy course control approval mechanisms in addition to their own institutional decision-making processes? The whole question of the role of validating bodies and course approval mechanisms requires review in the light of the claims for increasing autonomy being made on behalf of public sector institutions.

A final matter of concern is how higher education policies are generated. Since the 1960s DES policy making and effectiveness has been subject to criticism. There are many arguments as to where any blame lies, whether at ministerial or at civil servant level. It is clear that the development of higher education has over the years lacked the important ingredient of effective policy analysis. A much more consistent and determined approach will be required in future to the consideration of various policy options across the whole field of post-compulsory education. Steps should be taken to set up a higher education policy studies centre. It need have no formal powers but should derive its influence from the quality of its reports and the extent to which its work affects the day-to-day decisions that have to be taken in the DES, in the UGC, in the NAB, and within the institutions of higher education. The costs of such an enterprise would not be great and would be considerably outweighed by the long-term benefit to the system of expert analysis of policy options and the generation of informed comment on the development of policy. Government and the higher education authorities are in urgent need of informed policy analysis if the pattern of higher education we have today is to be adapted to the needs of the later 1980s and 1990s.

Proposals

1. The DES, the UGC and the NAB should recognize that the protection and encouragement of institutional self-governance and initiative through the operation of multiple sources of funding, responsiveness to external societal demands and strong local/community involvement offer the best prospect for maintaining academic innovation and creativity.

2. Greater emphasis should be given to institutional autonomy. Autonomy, however, should be regulated by agreed institutional 'mission statements' and considerations of national need and the patterns of demand. Funding should be in accordance with institutions' mission statements, which should be the subject of periodic review.

3. Representative local committees should be set up to co-ordinate and stimulate the provision of adult, continuing and post-experience education, combining the interests of institutions, LEAs and other local providers.

4. Machinery for co-operation at regional level amongst institutions of higher education should be set up by the institutions themselves to complement the closer working relationships between the UGC and the NAB recommended below (Proposal 11).

5. Priority should be given to adopting systems of course control which encourage academic initiative and speedy responses to changing student interests.

6. The UGC and the NAB should place a high priority on the need for co-operation at officer, committee/board and subject committee levels.

7. UGC and NAB advice to government should be published, as should the criteria they use to make judgements between institutions.

8. The staffing of the two bodies should be adequate to their respective remits and should be appointed independently of the DES, a majority being drawn from higher education itself.

9. Ways should be found, either by the appointment of assessors on the committee/board or at the subject committee level, of relating the legitimate interests of government departments other than the DES with the work of UGC/NAB and with the institutions of higher education, in order to ensure that institutions' research and training responsibilities take proper account of national needs.

10 The Secretary of State should continue to appoint members of the UGC, but should publish the criteria governing the selection in advance and should take the necessary decision only after consultation with the various constituencies involved, including the consumers of higher education.

11 After a five-year review period, the longer-term prospect should be for an even closer working relationship between UGC and NAB, and that the two bodies and the DES should accept this as their long-term objective.

12 UGC and NAB should include within their remit the entire higher education provision including direct grant and voluntary institutions.

13 In any future arrangements there should be a recognition and reflection of a continuing place for LEAs in tertiary education provision.

14 The role of validating bodies in the future structure of higher education needs review as their role changes in respect to the increasingly autonomous institutions in the public sector.

15 An overarching advisory body should be established to offer strategic advice to the Secretary of State on matters relating to higher education including the division of funding. The new body should not interfere with the established powers and functions of the UGC and NAB.

16 Priority should be given to the establishment of a higher education policy studies centre to serve as an independent source of advice for the DES and other government departments as well as the UGC, NAB and the institutions of higher education themselves.

ACKNOWLEDGEMENTS

We wish to express our appreciation to the Governing Council of the Society for Research into Higher Education and to the Leverhulme Trust: the one for their foresight in promoting such a programme of study well before the expenditure cuts of 1981; the other for their most generous financial support. Additional financial suport was given by the Gulbenkian Foundation and by the DES to further our work on the arts in higher education and on resources and their allocation.

This has been a very wide-ranging programme and many hundreds of individuals have contributed to it through attendance at meetings and submission of written evidence. They are acknowledged in the respective specialized volumes. The list below is of others who have made formal contributions but who have not yet been acknowledged elsewhere. None of them is responsible for our interpretation of their advice.

SRHE Working Party 1979 - 1981 Donald Bligh, Charles Carter, Colin Flood-Page, Harriet Greenaway, Richard Griffiths, Roy Niblett, Peter Scott and Michael Shattock.

Research Advisory Group 1981 - 1982 Ron Barnett, Donald Bligh, Peter Brinson, Rowland Eustace, Oliver Fulton, Maurice Kogan, Robert Lindley, Alfred Morris, Roy Niblett, Geoffrey Oldham, Ken Robinson, Michael Shattock, John Sizer and Leslie Wagner.

Organizers of conferences Peter Ayscough, John Davies, Lewis Elton, Trevor Habeshaw, Ian Gibbs, Robin Plummer, Ernest Rudd, Graham Stodd and David Walker.

Organizations and individuals providing written material Association of Graduate Careers Advisory Services, Association of Metropolitan Authorities, Association of Polytechnic Teachers, Association of University Teachers, Chartered Institute of Public Finance and Accountancy, Committee of Polytechnic Directors, Committee of Vice-Chancellors and Principals, Council for Educational Technology, Council for National

Academic Awards, Confederation of British Industry, Council for Local Education Authorities, T.E. Dean, Department of Industry, Design Council, Institute of Manpower Studies, Gordon Miller, National Association of Teachers in Further and Higher Education, National Union of Students, Open University, D.J. Parsons, G.W. Prior-Wandesforde, Science and Engineering Research Council, Tom Schuller, Neil Scott, T. Snow, Standing Conference of Employers of Graduates, Standing Conference of Principals and Directors of Colleges and Institutes of Higher Education, Trades Union Congress.